I0696191

This Book Belongs to

About Mindful Zenith Publication

Mindful Zenith is a dynamic publishing company offering creative products suitable for all age groups. Our publications strive to bring happiness to readers and facilitate the easy assimilation of new knowledge. We are dedicated to enhancing each new release, actively seeking candid feedback from our cherished customers. Consider our books as delightful presents for yourself or your loved ones, ideal for holidays or any special celebration.

If you like our book, please leave us positive review on Amazon. Your support is the greatest motivation and compliment for us.

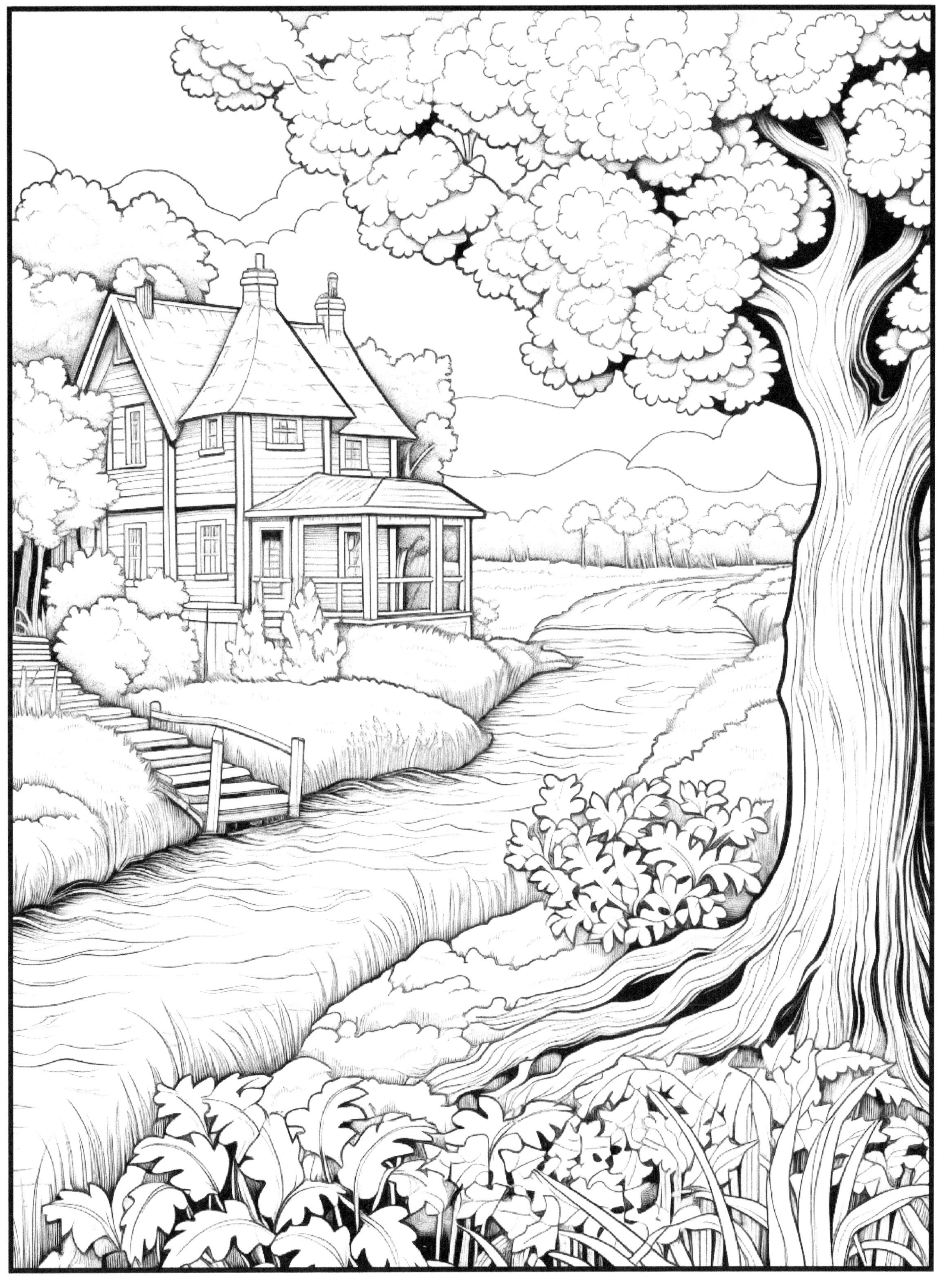

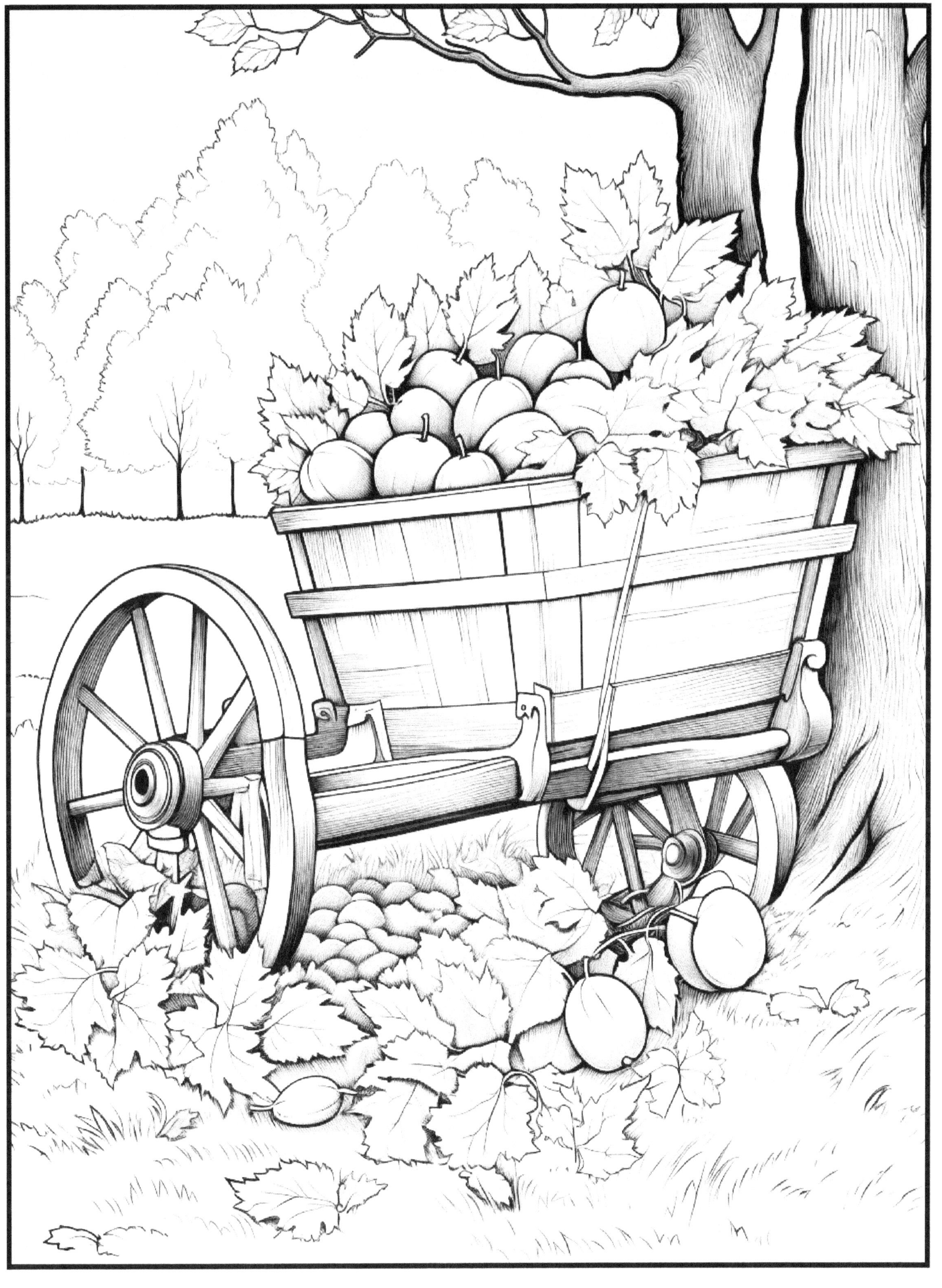

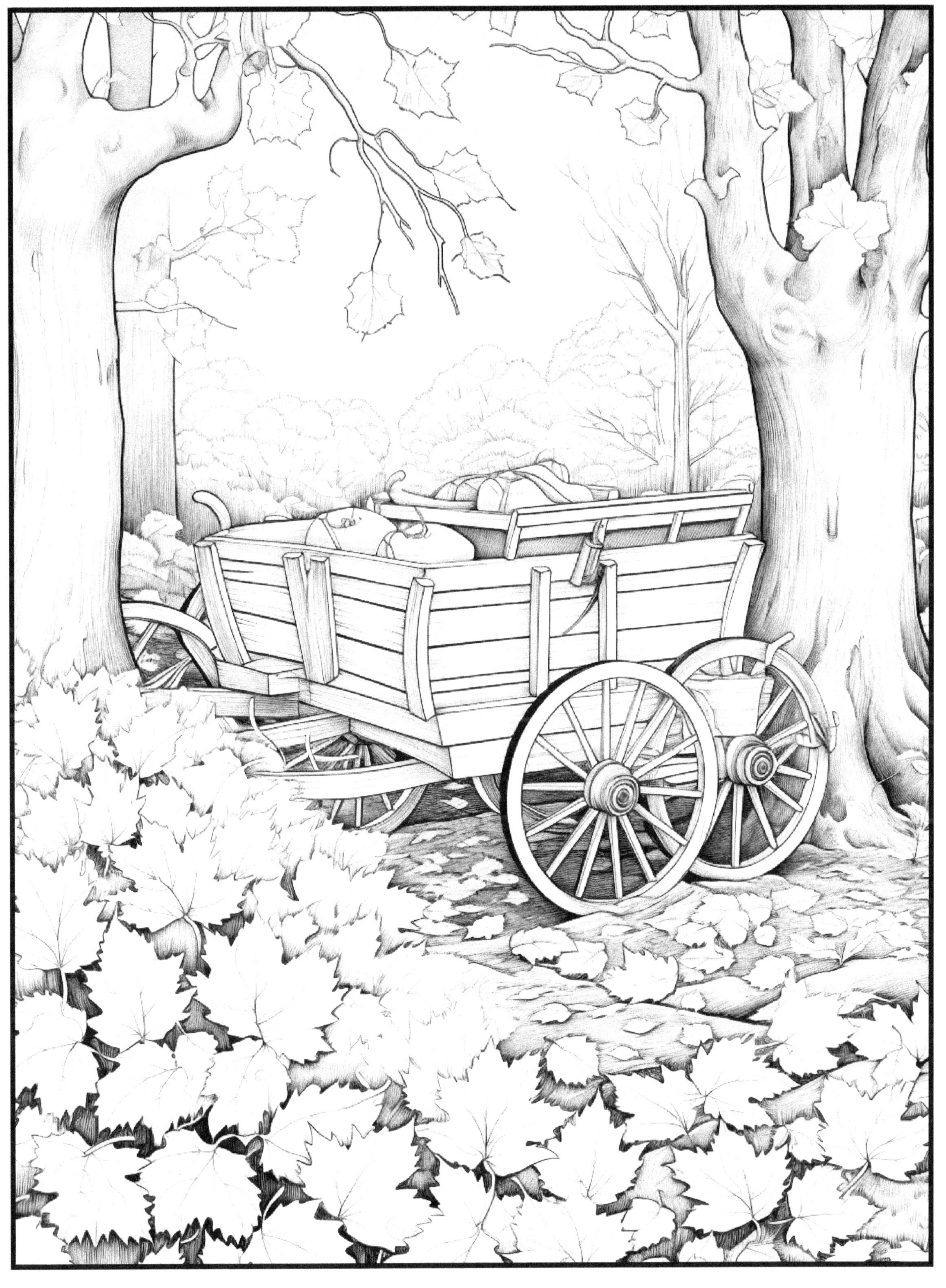

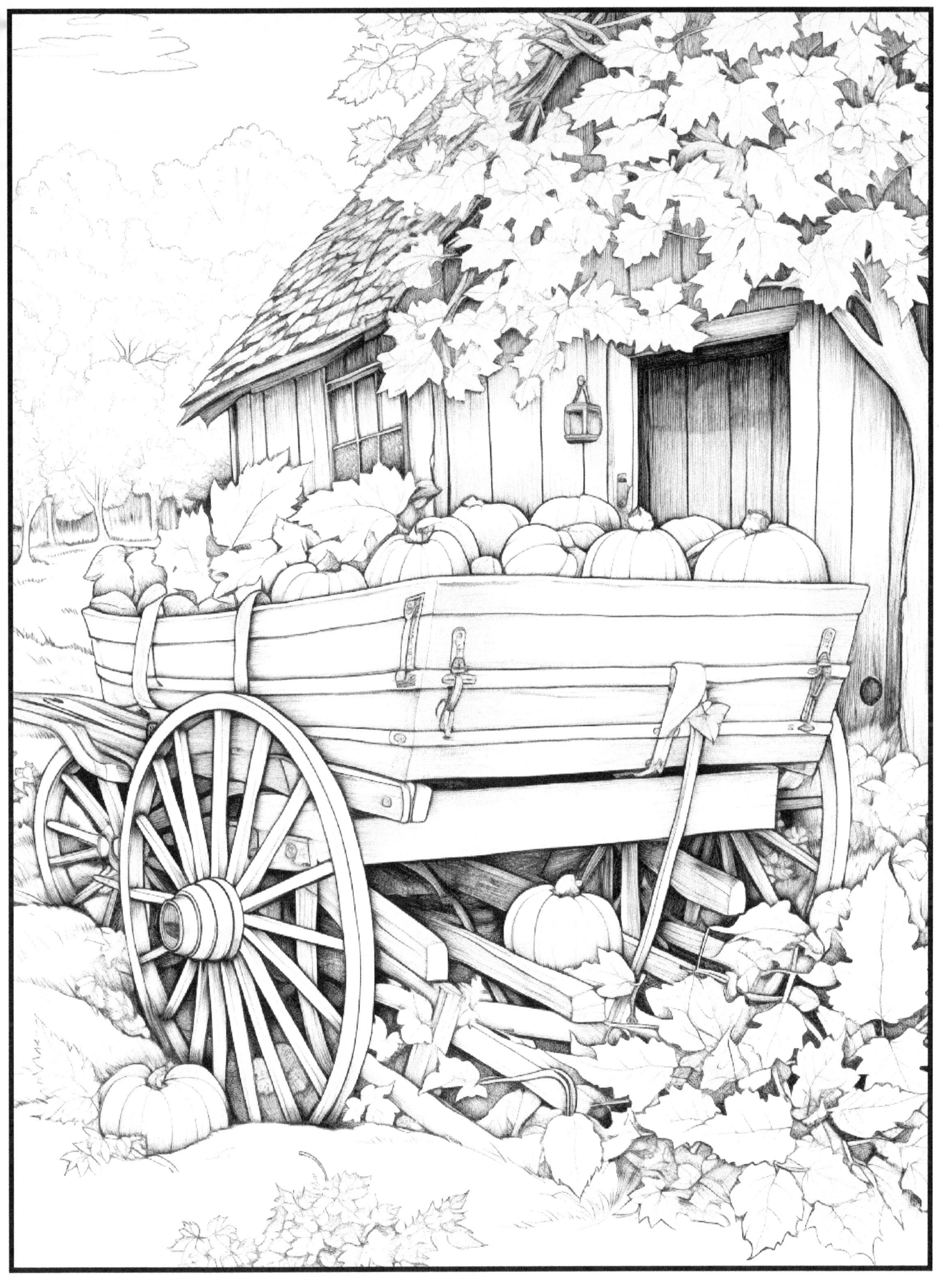

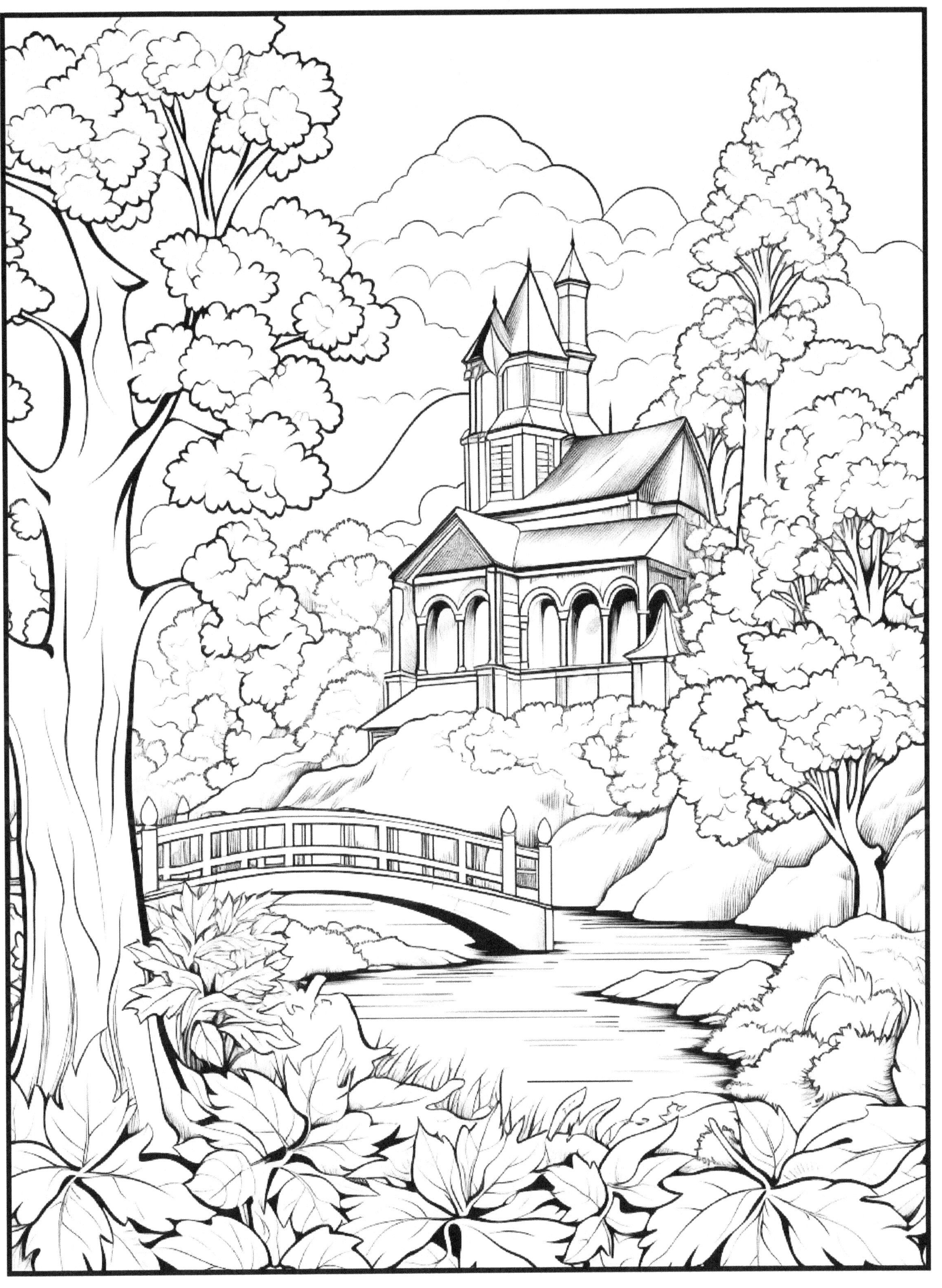

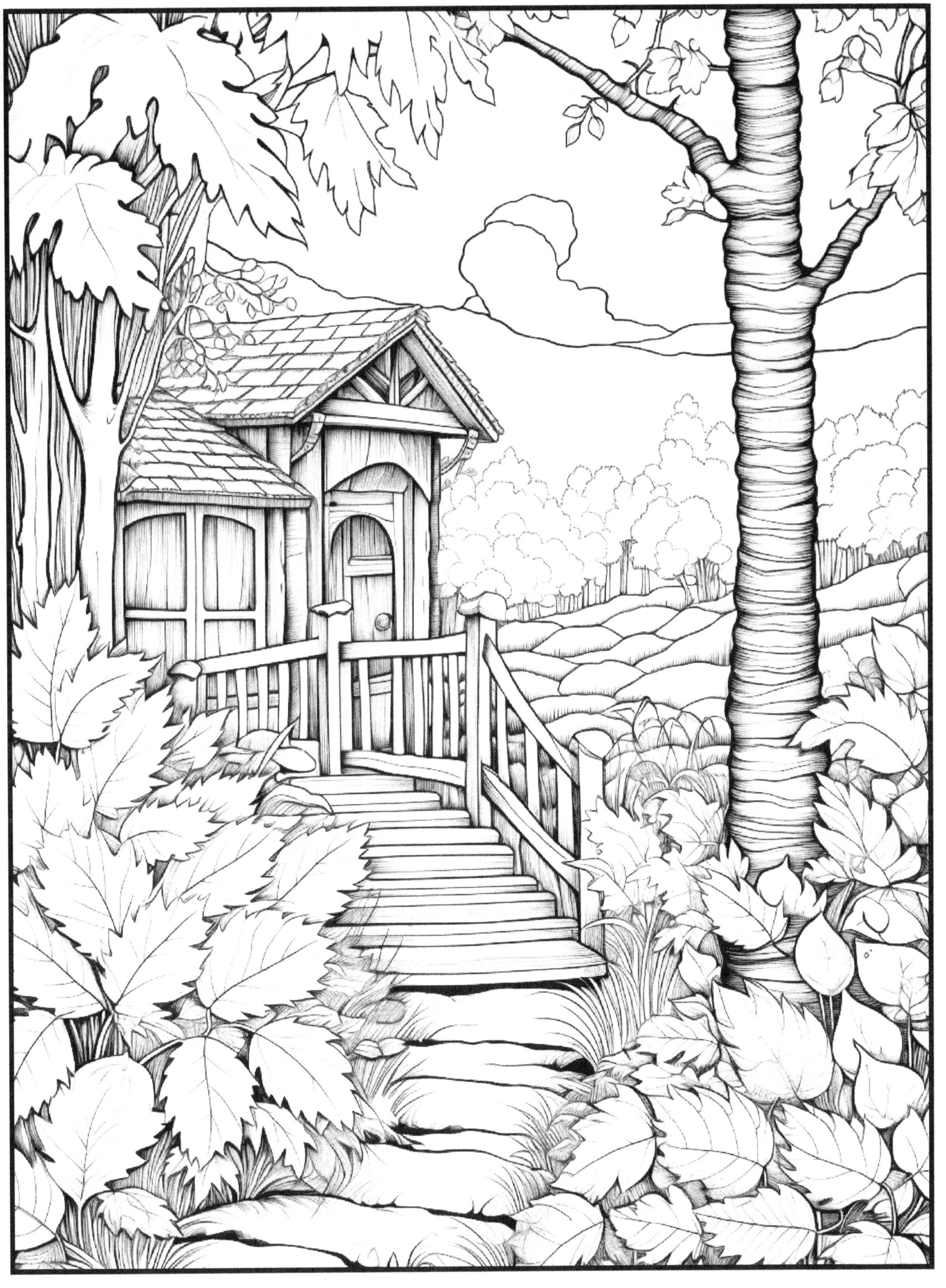

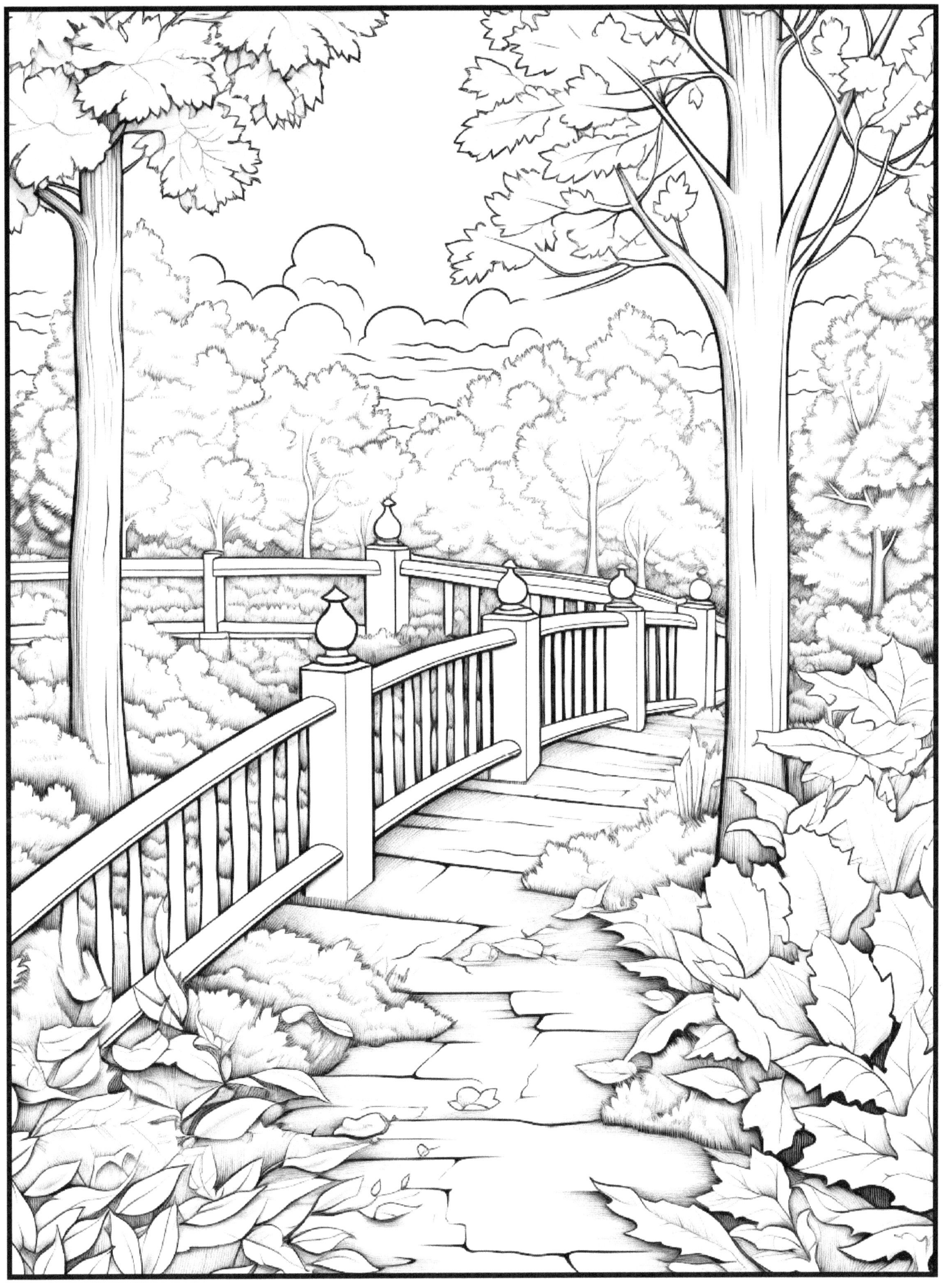

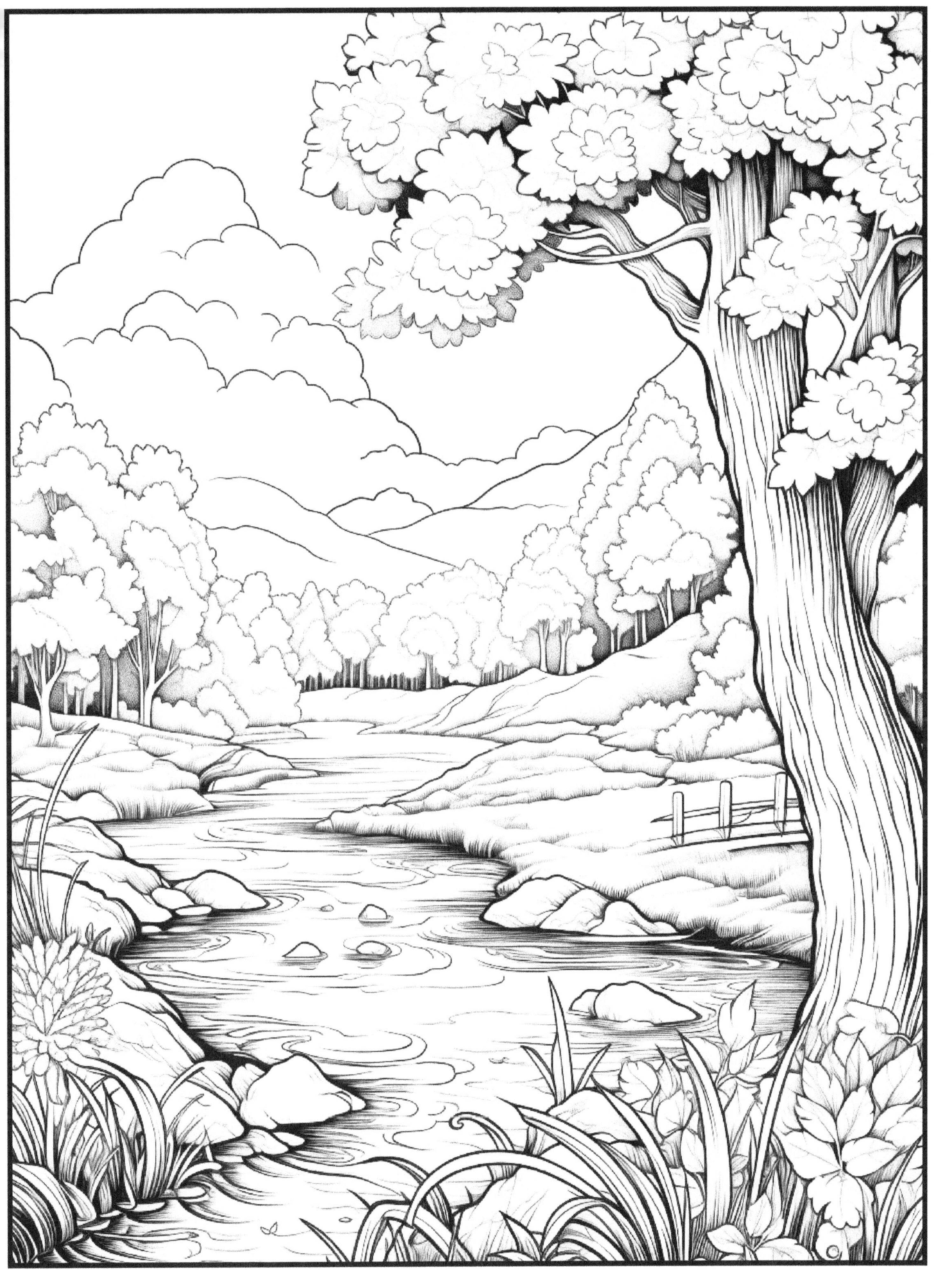

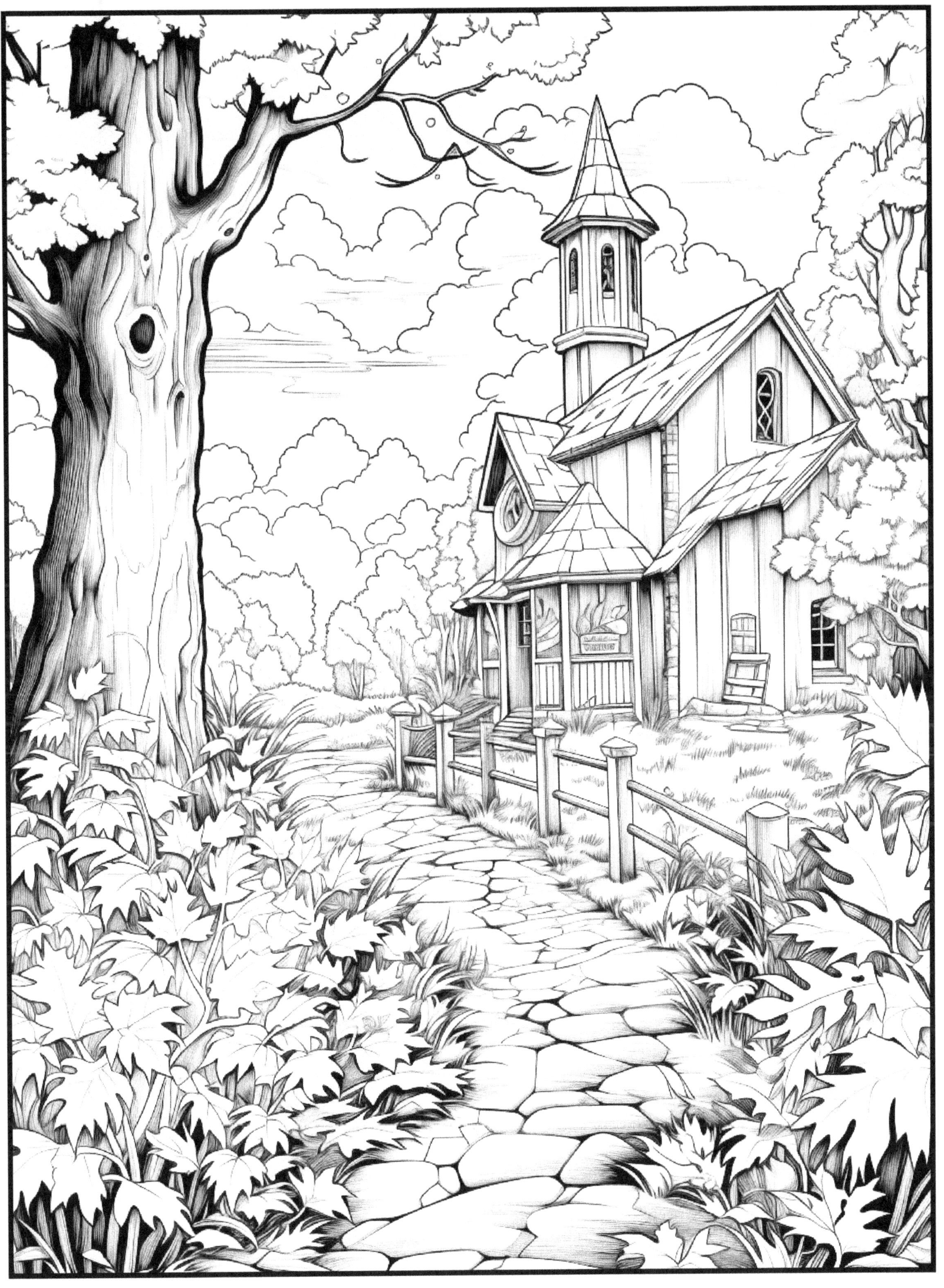

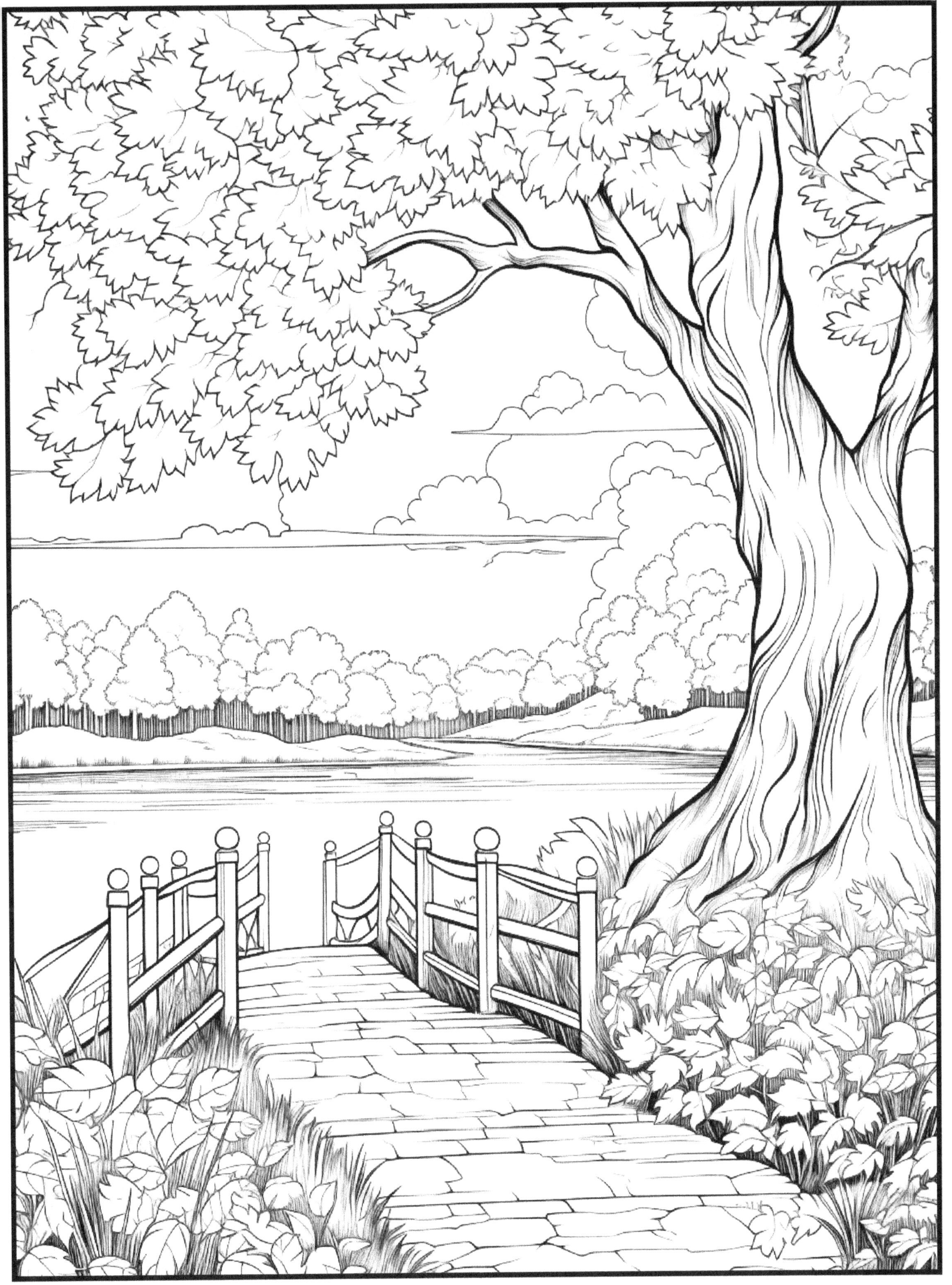

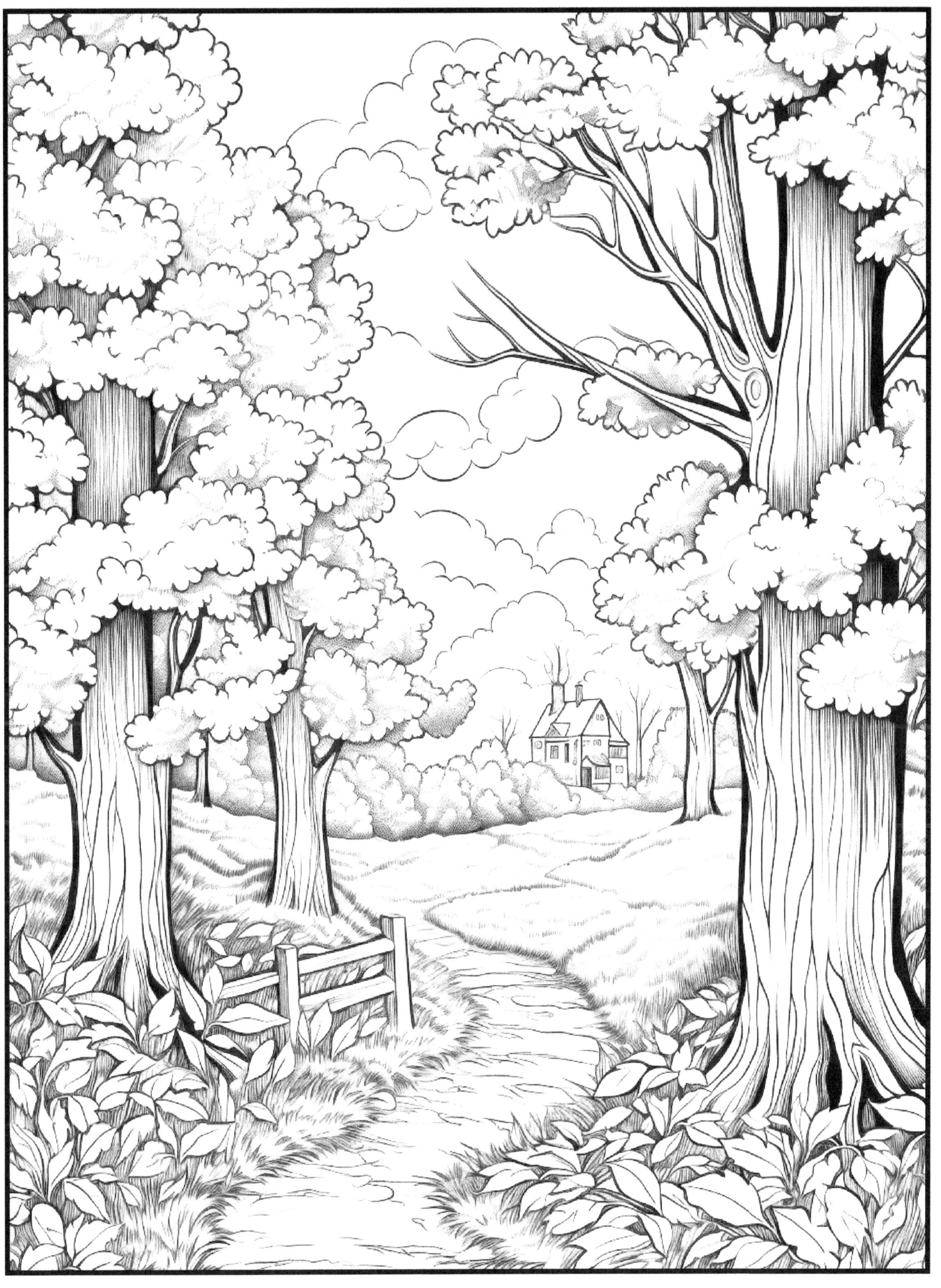

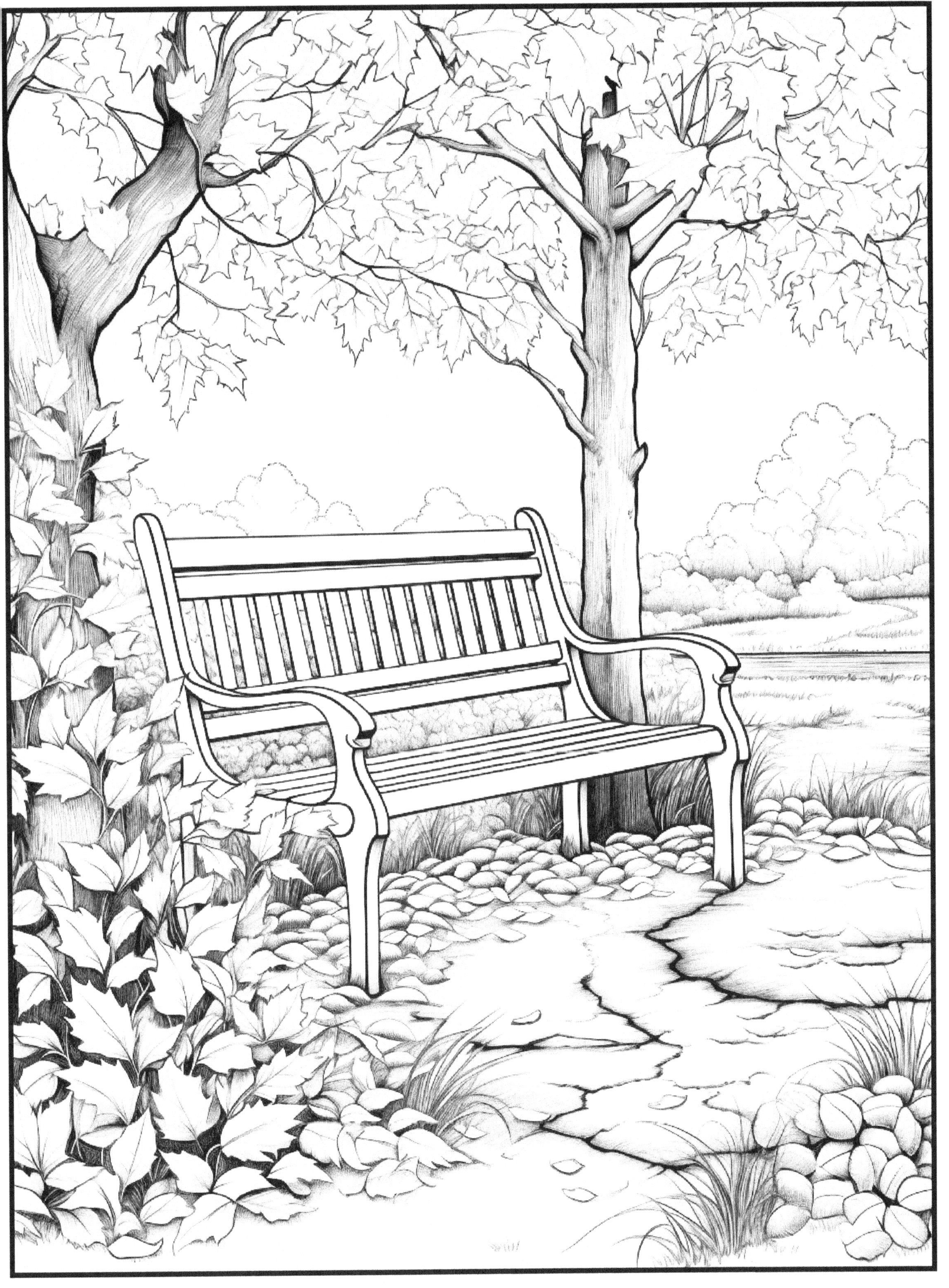

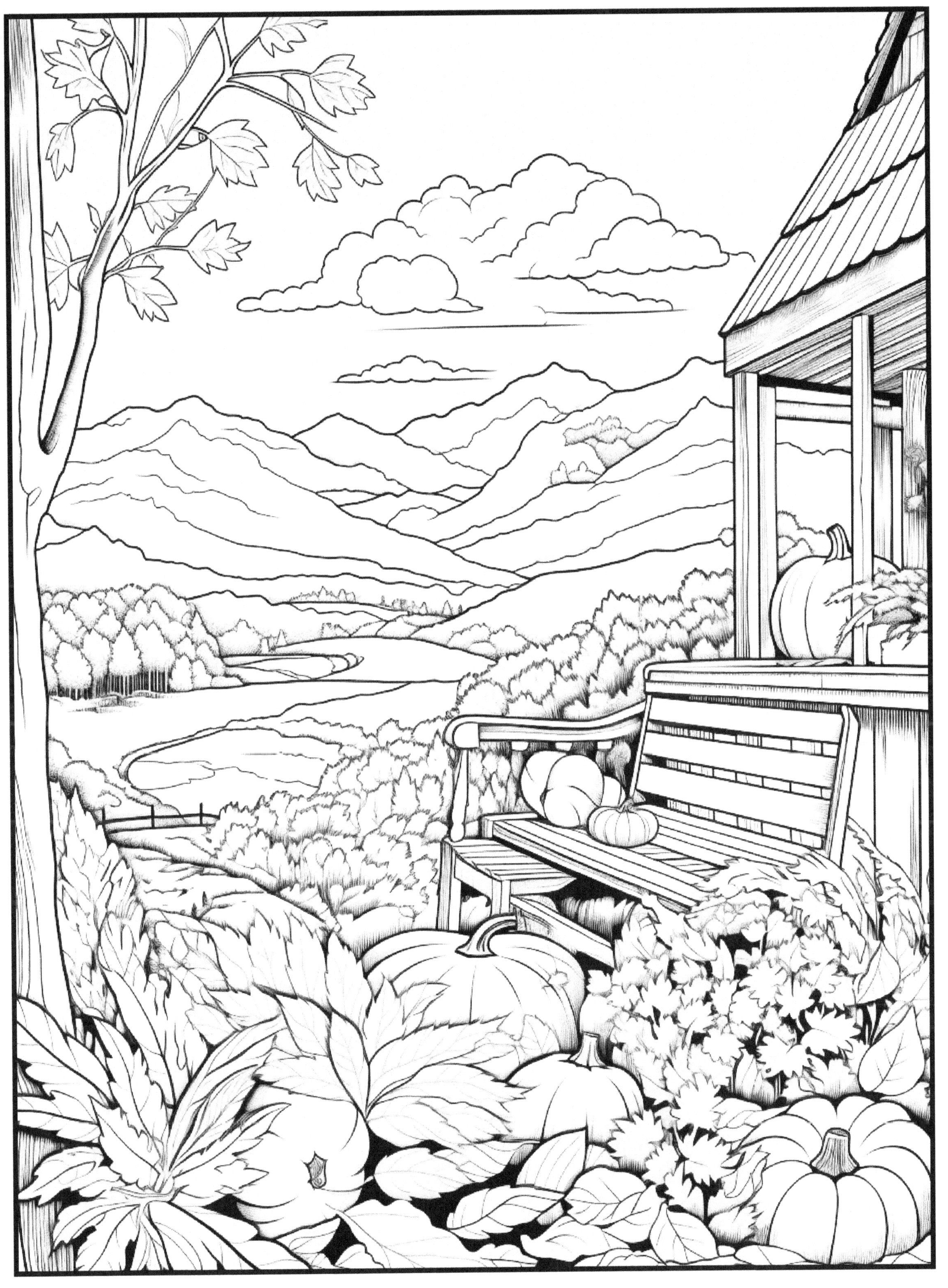

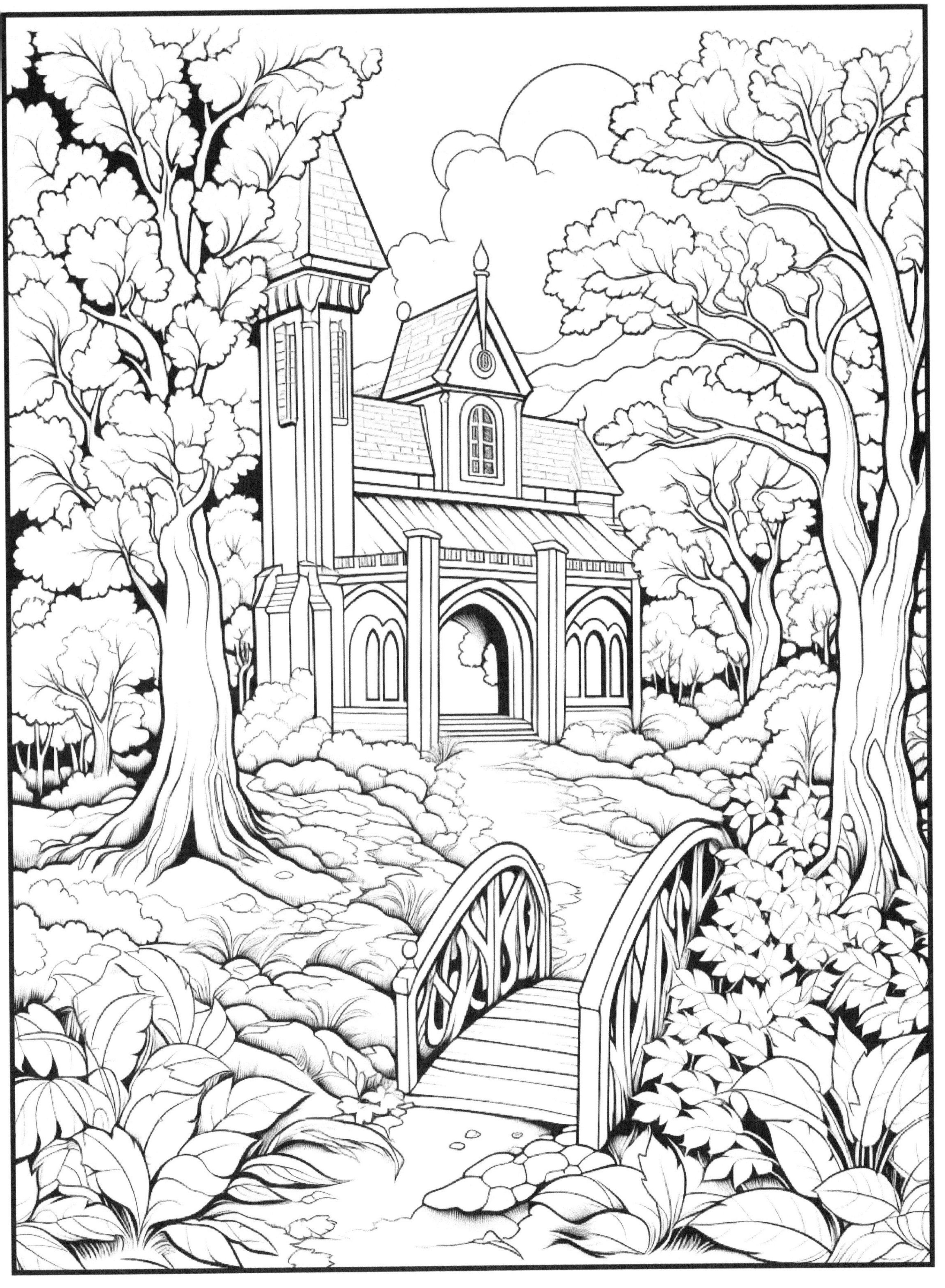

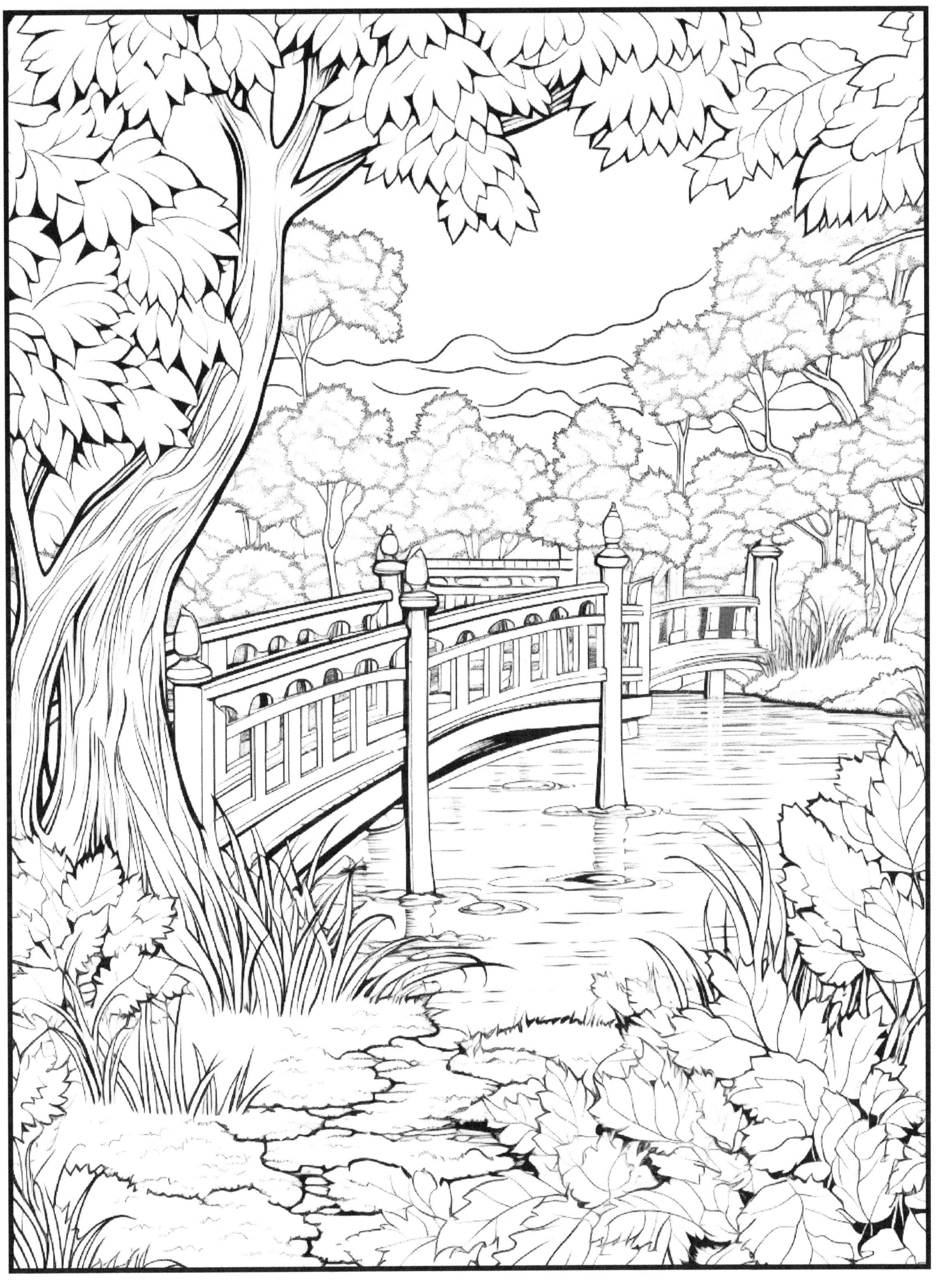

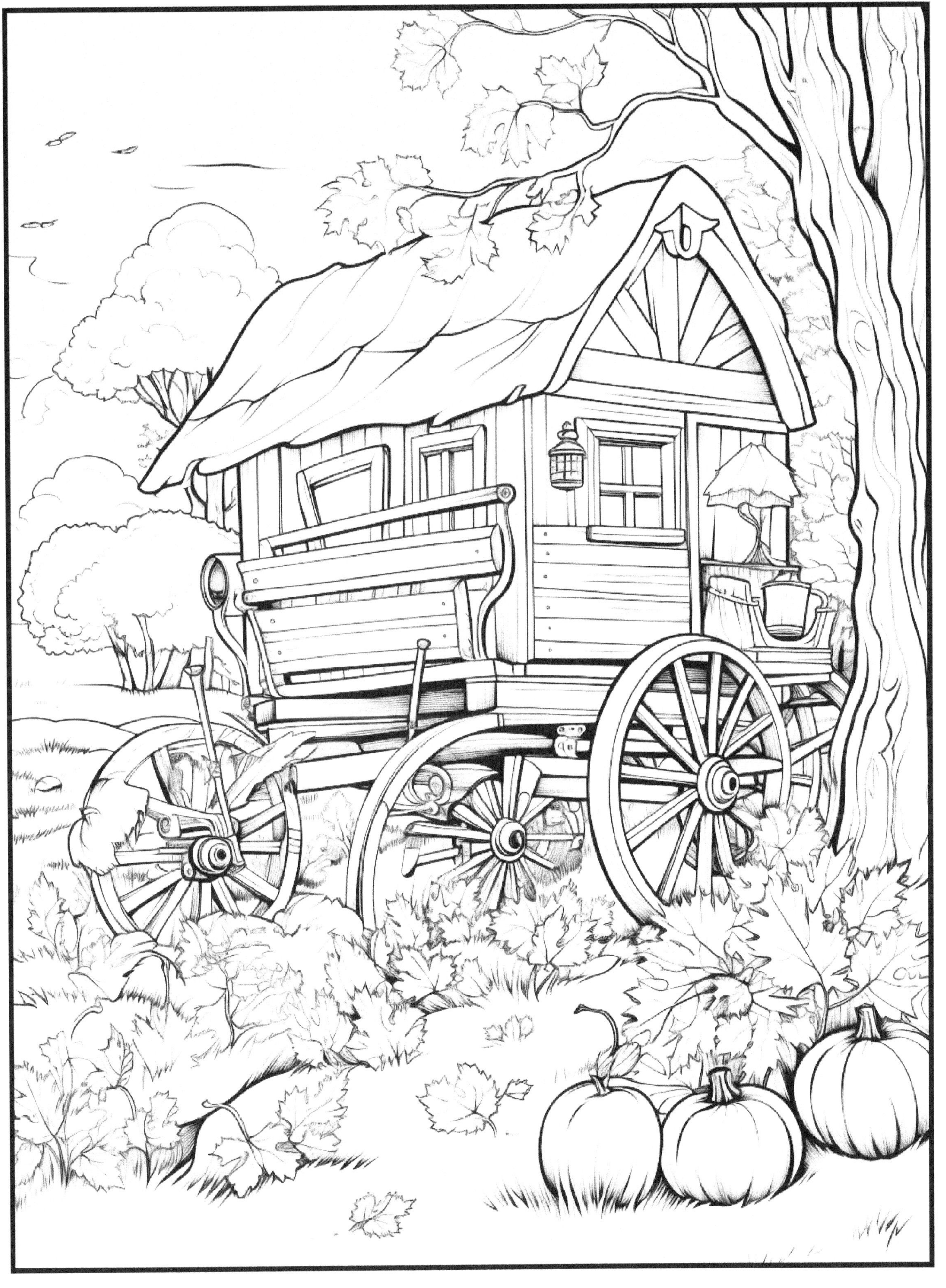

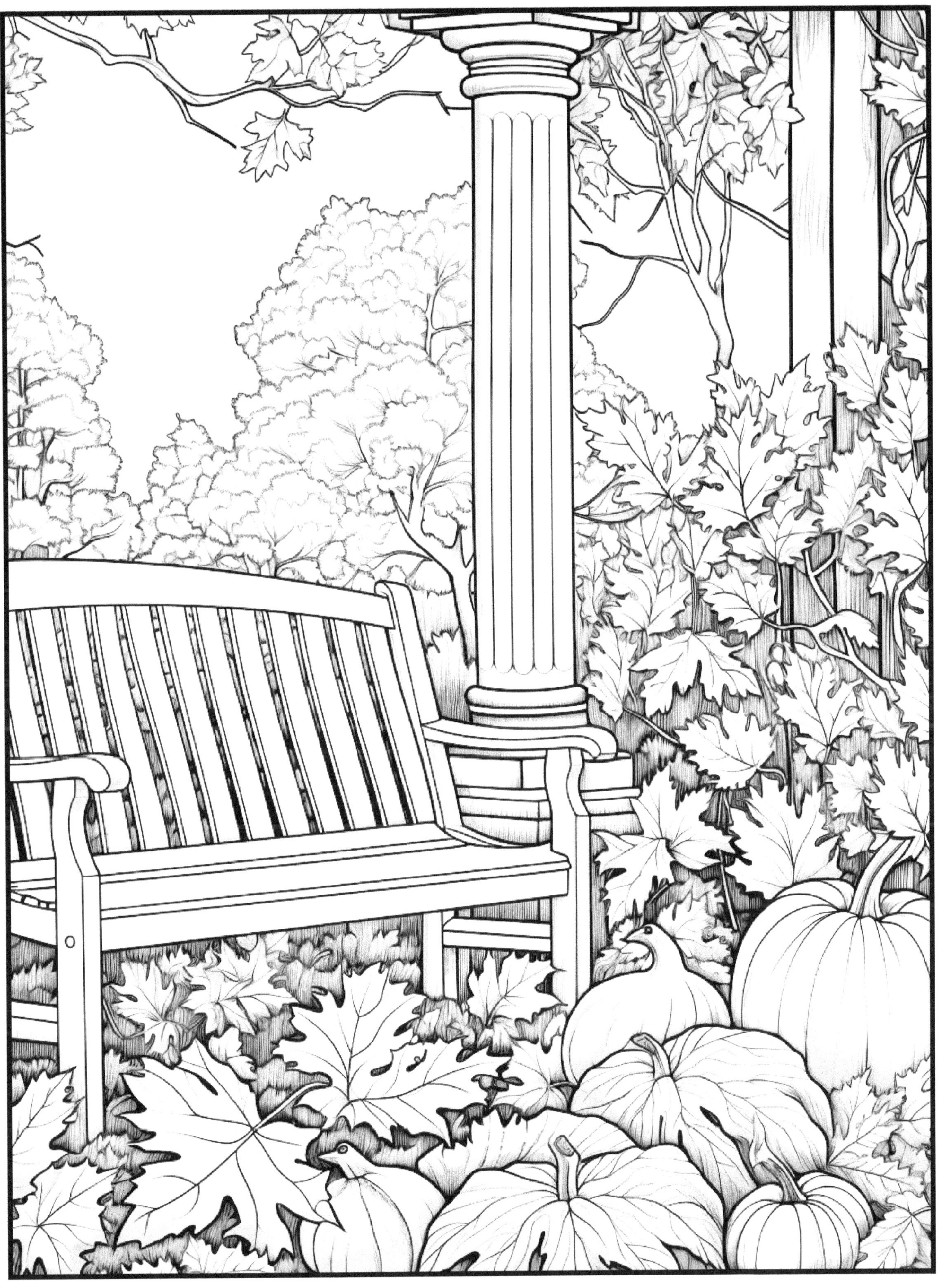

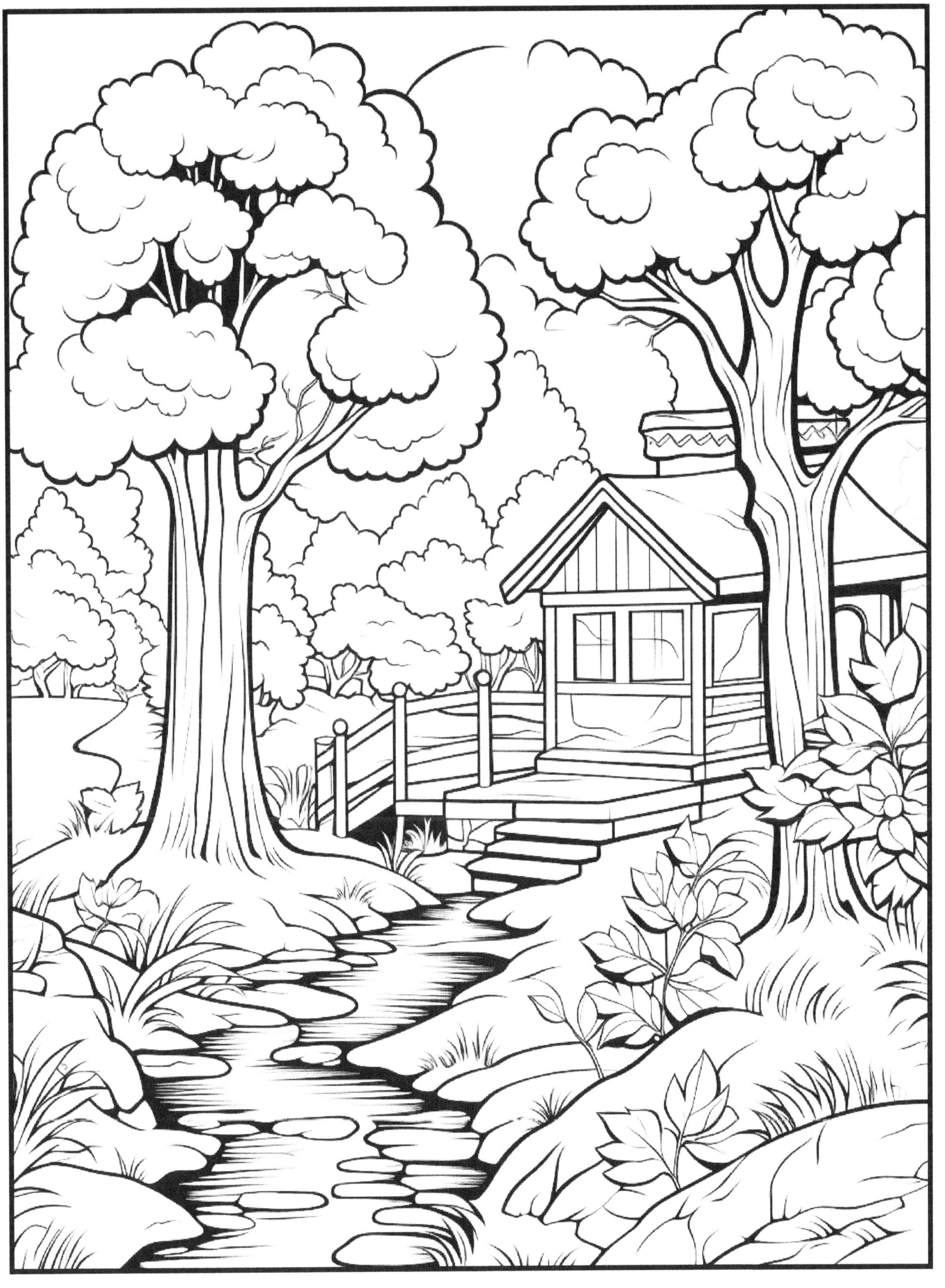

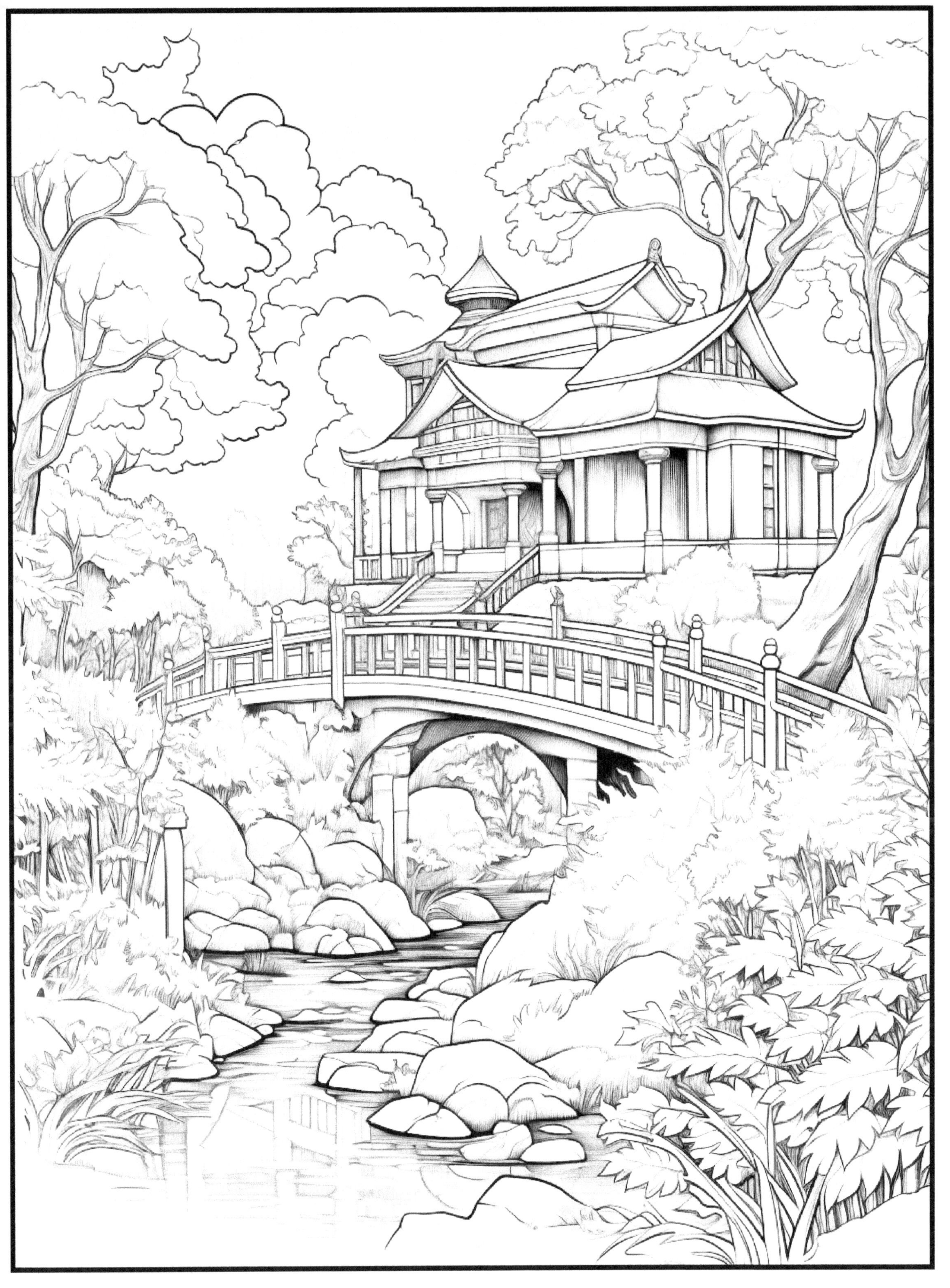

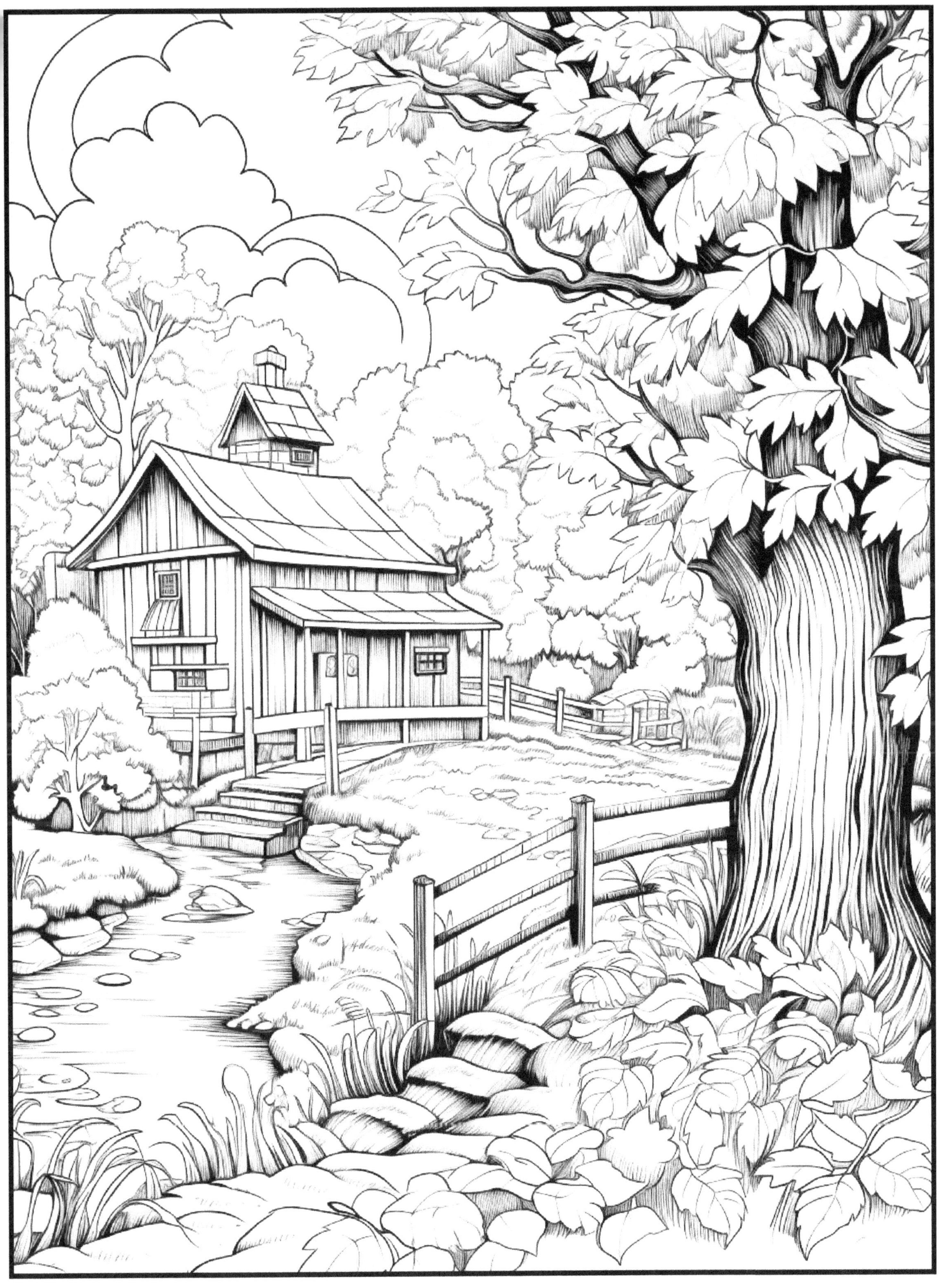

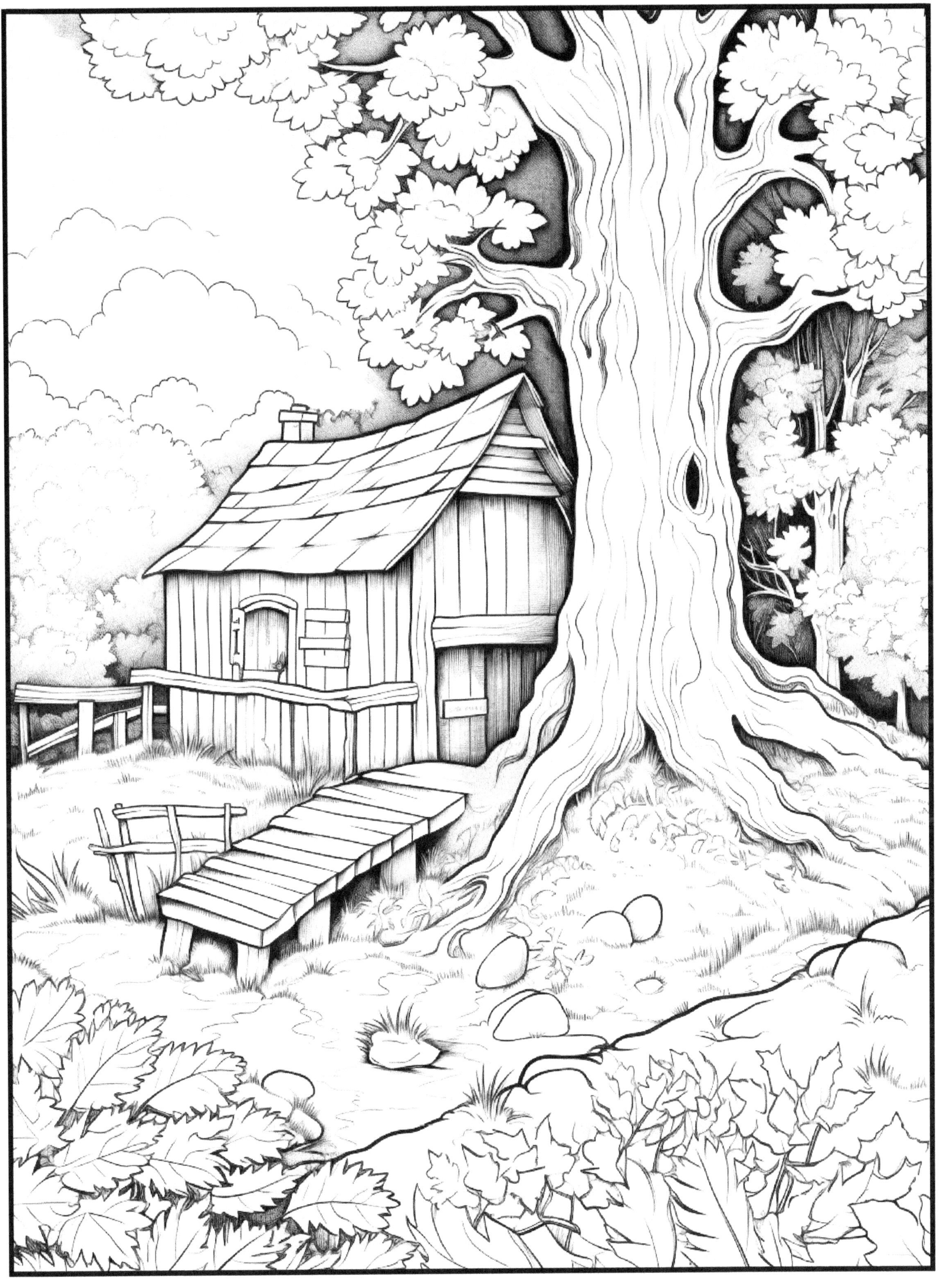

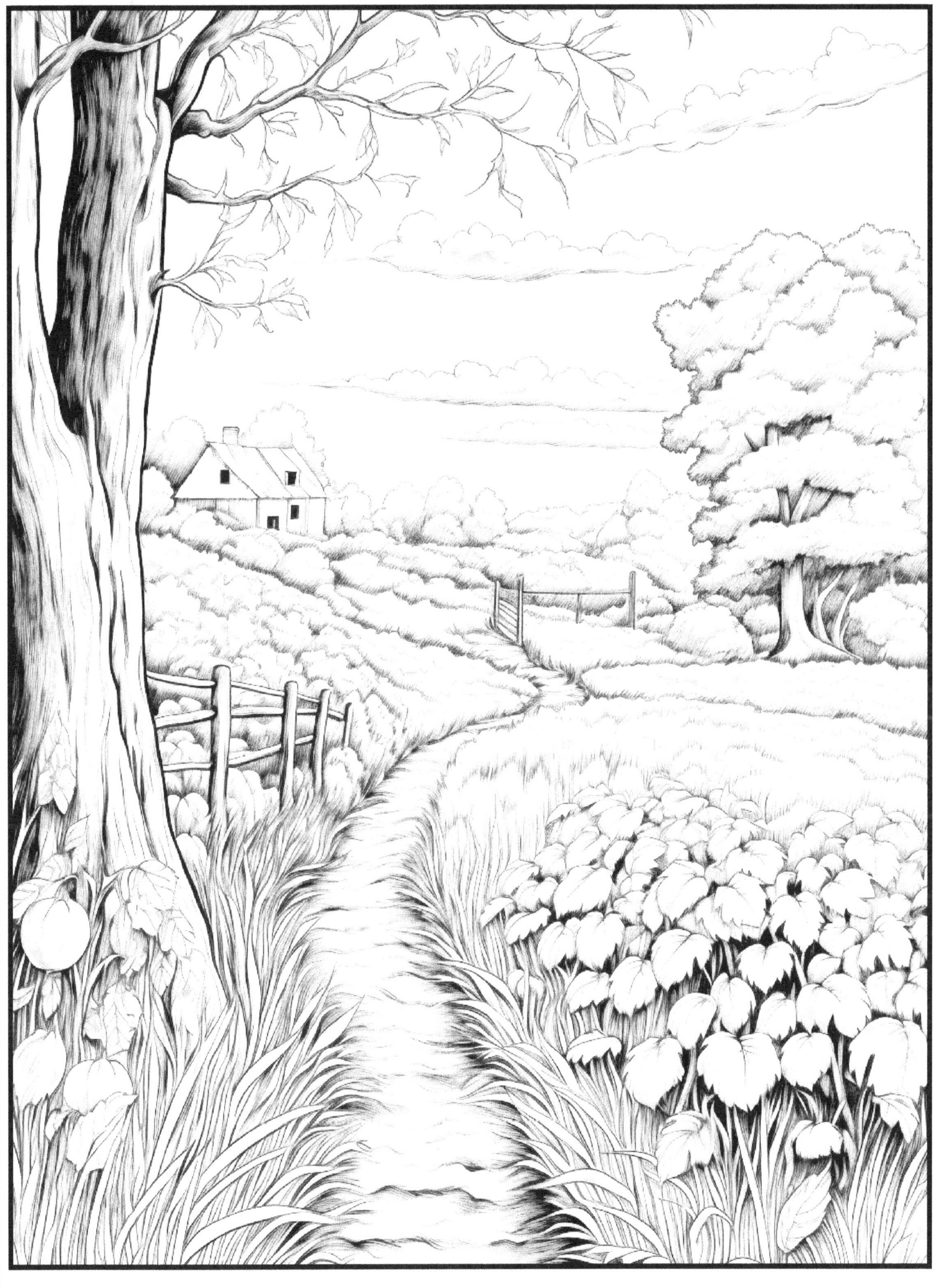

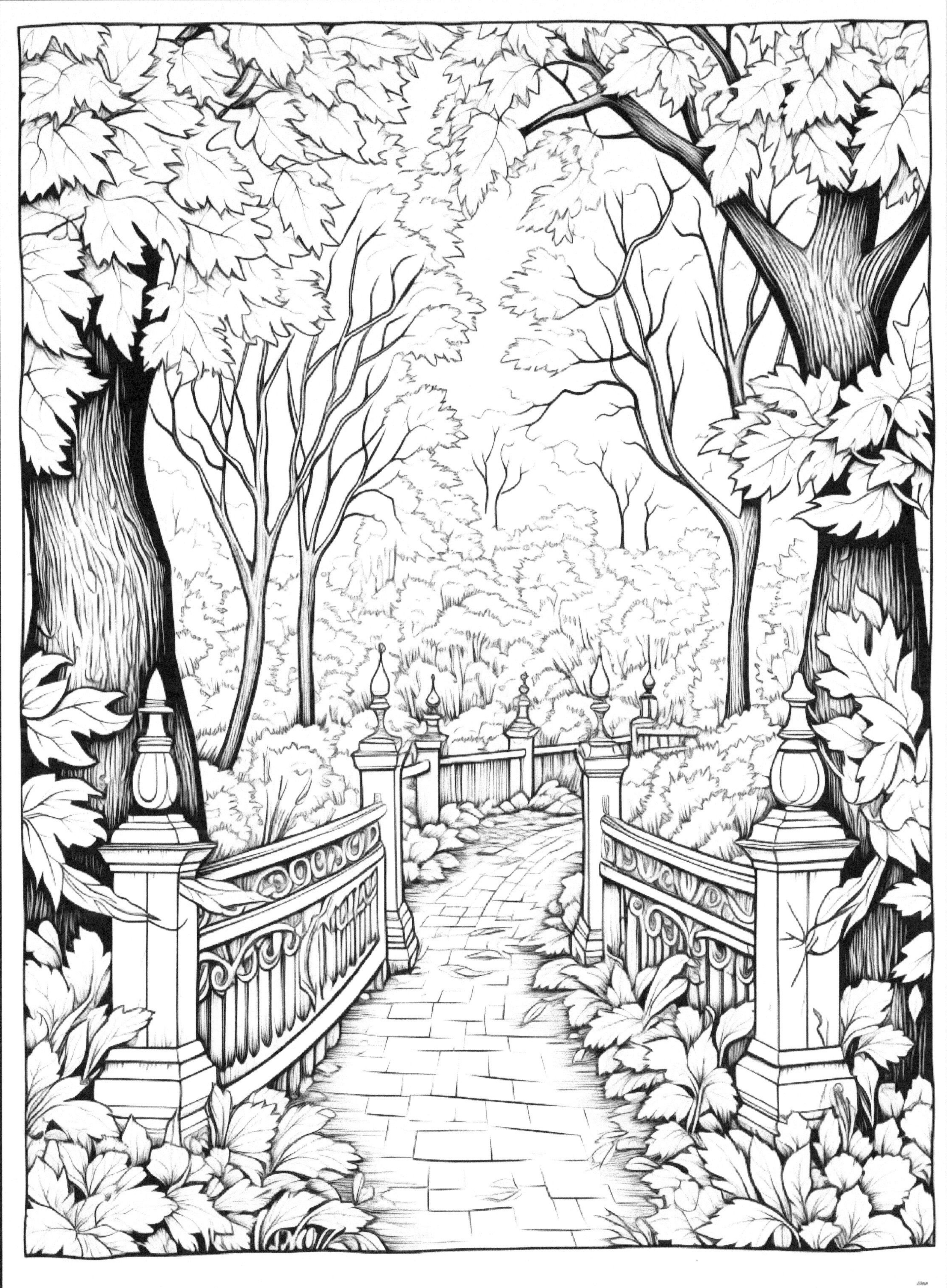

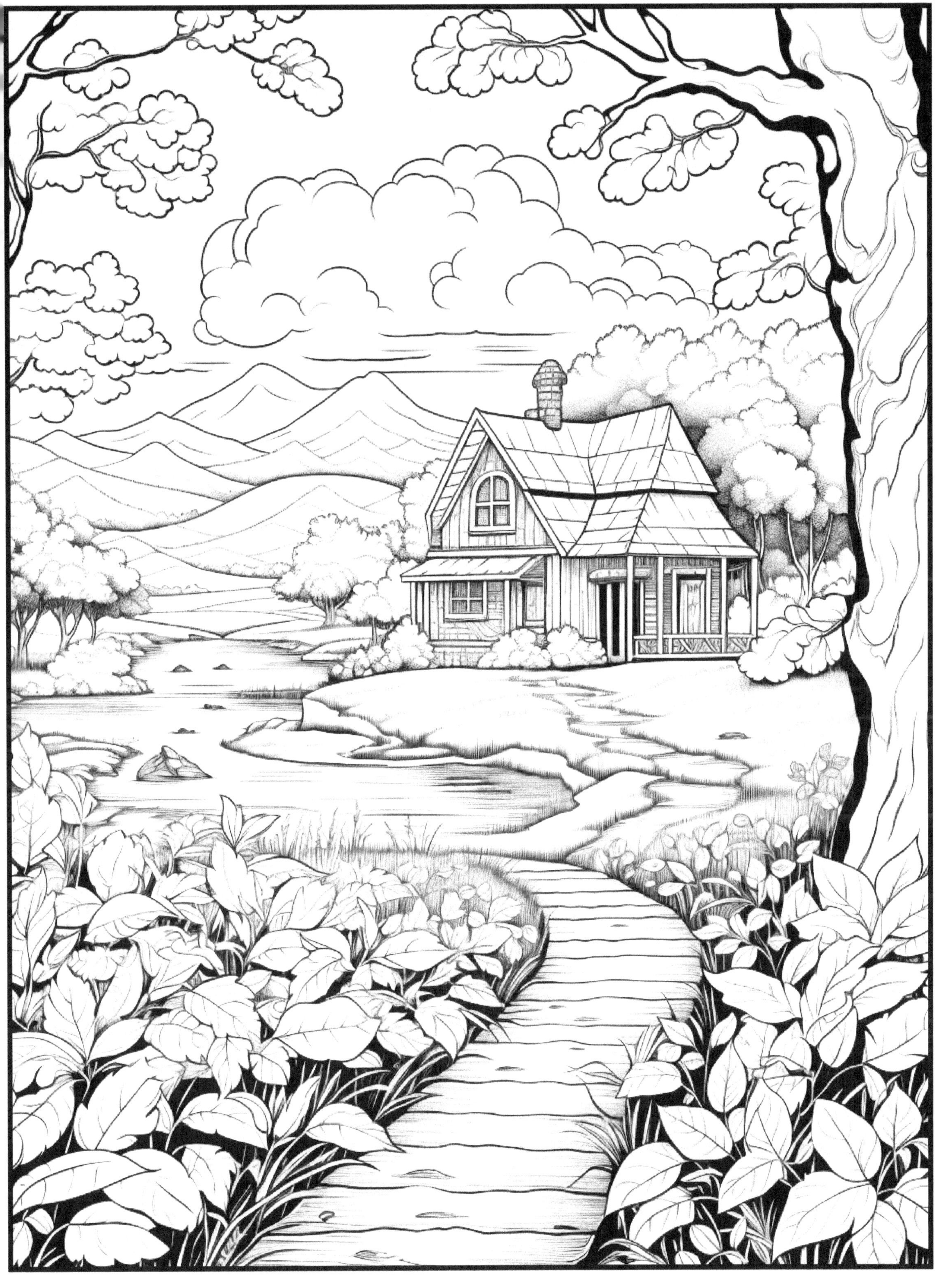

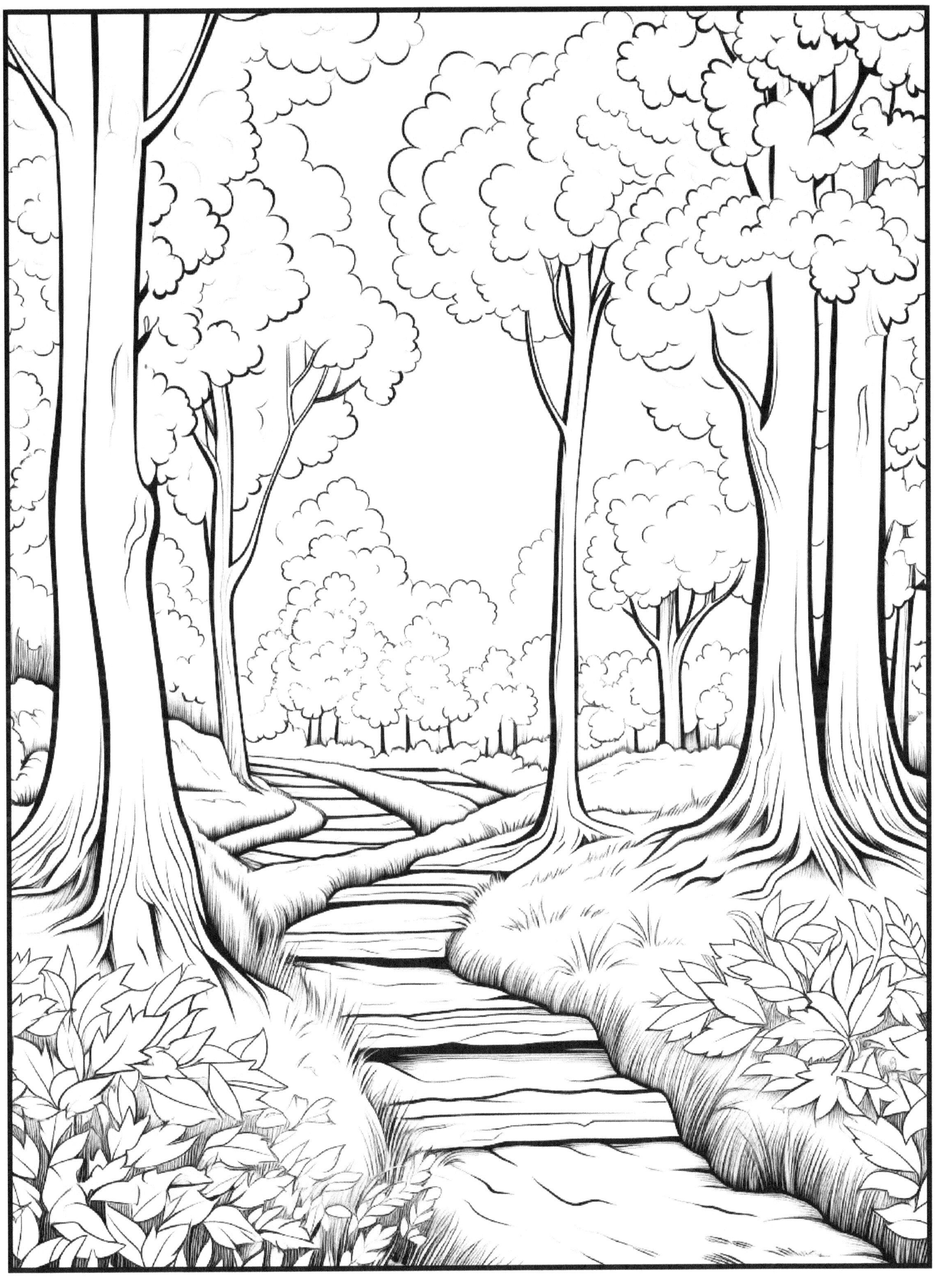

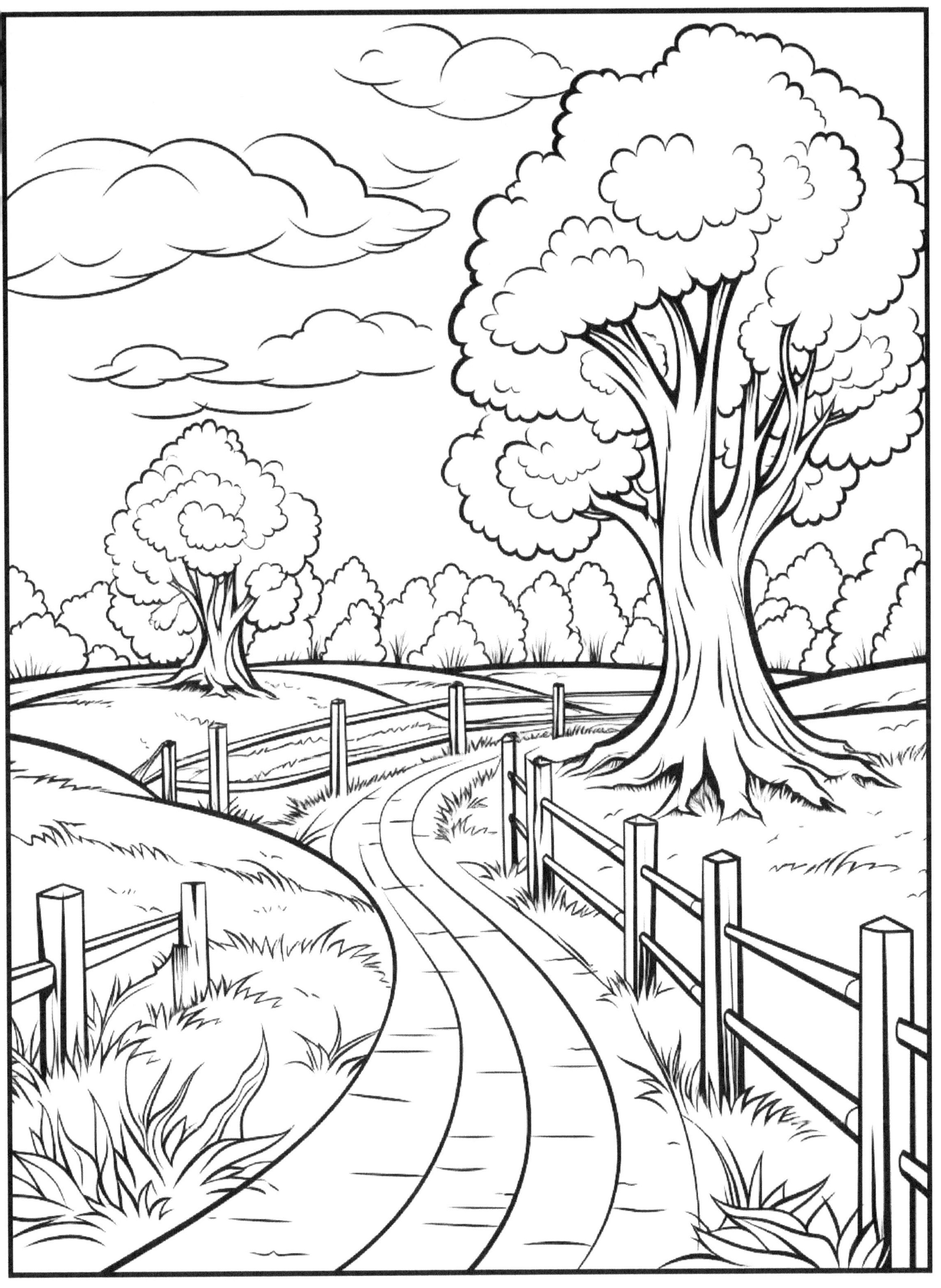

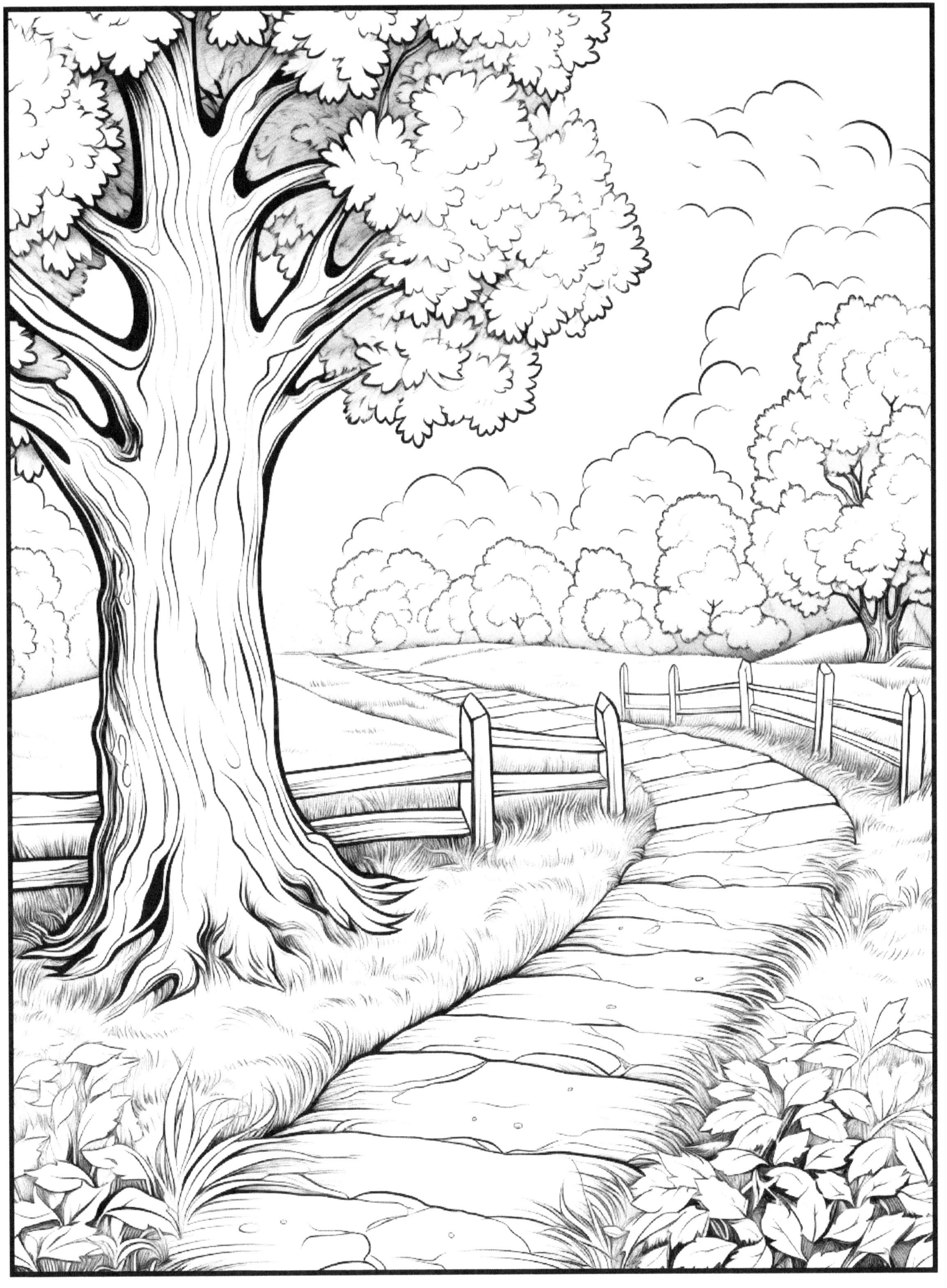

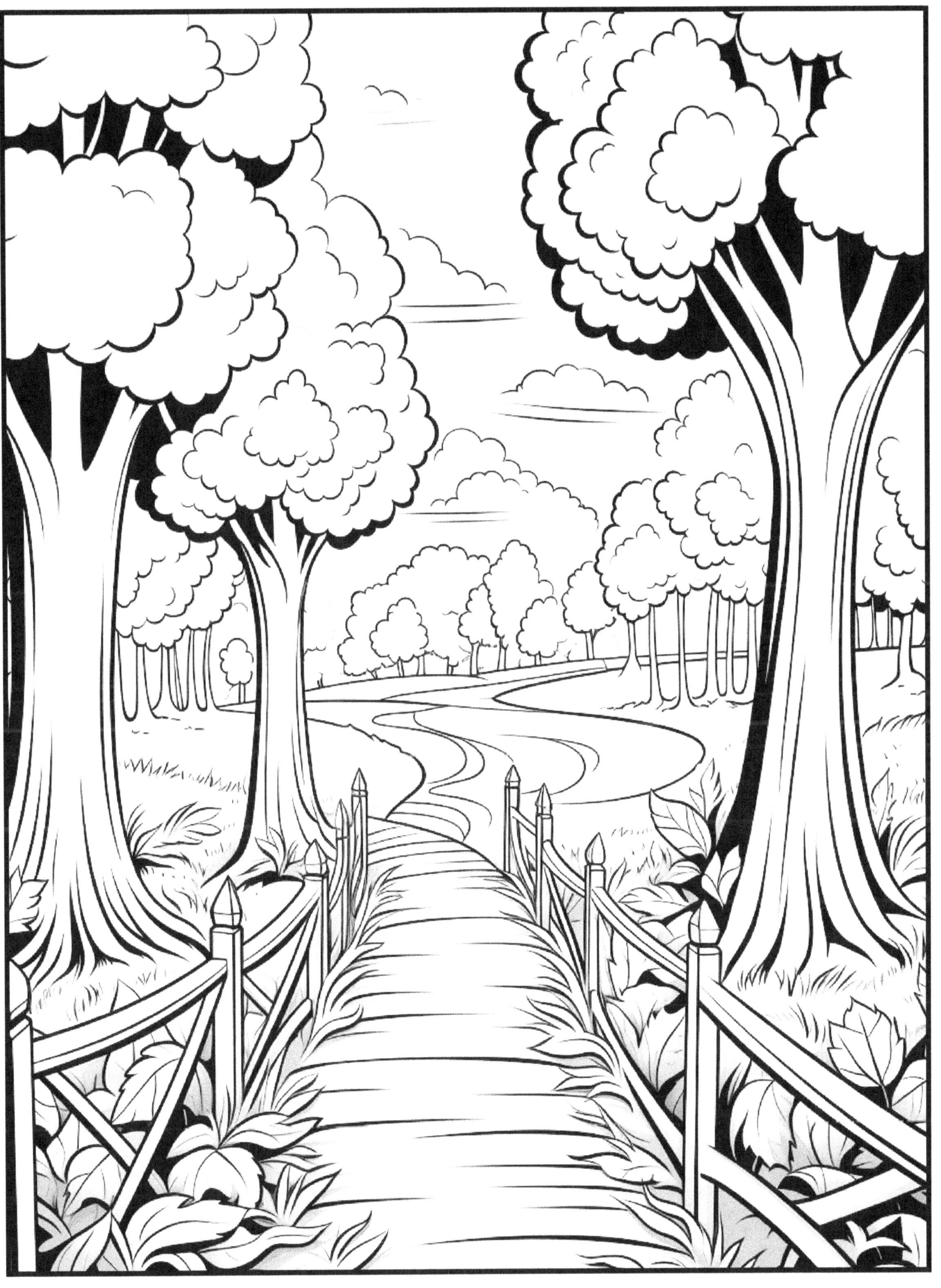

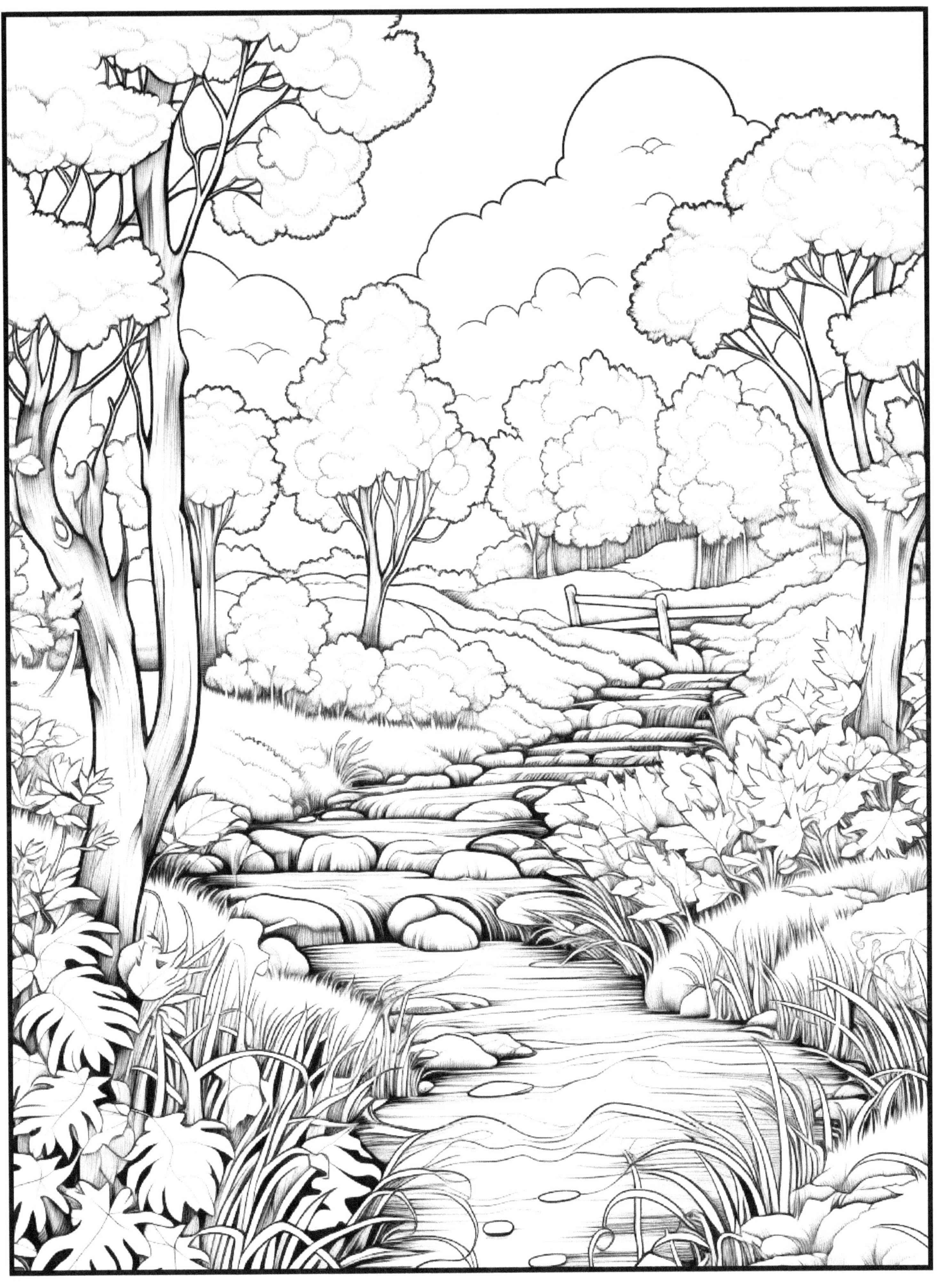

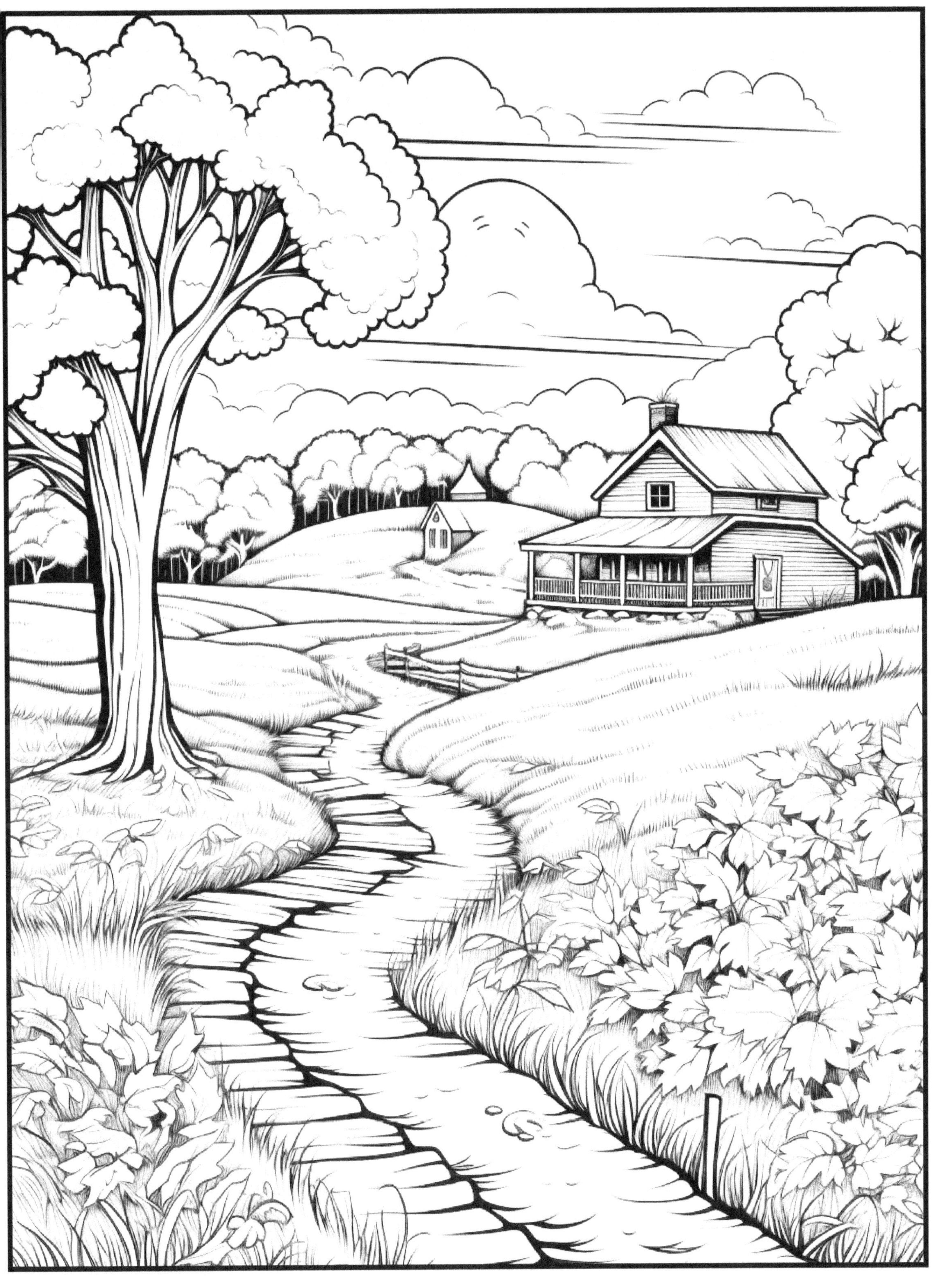

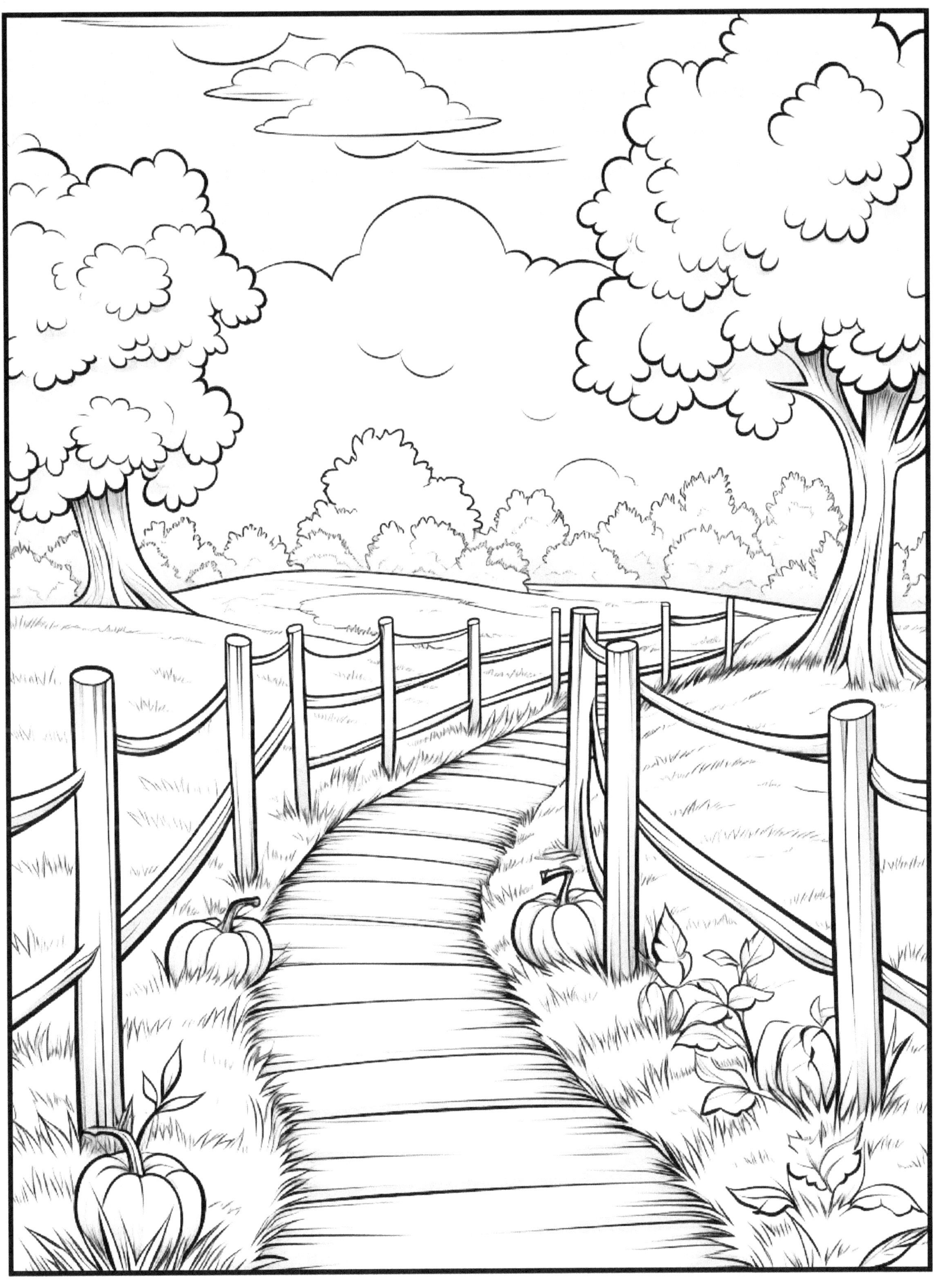

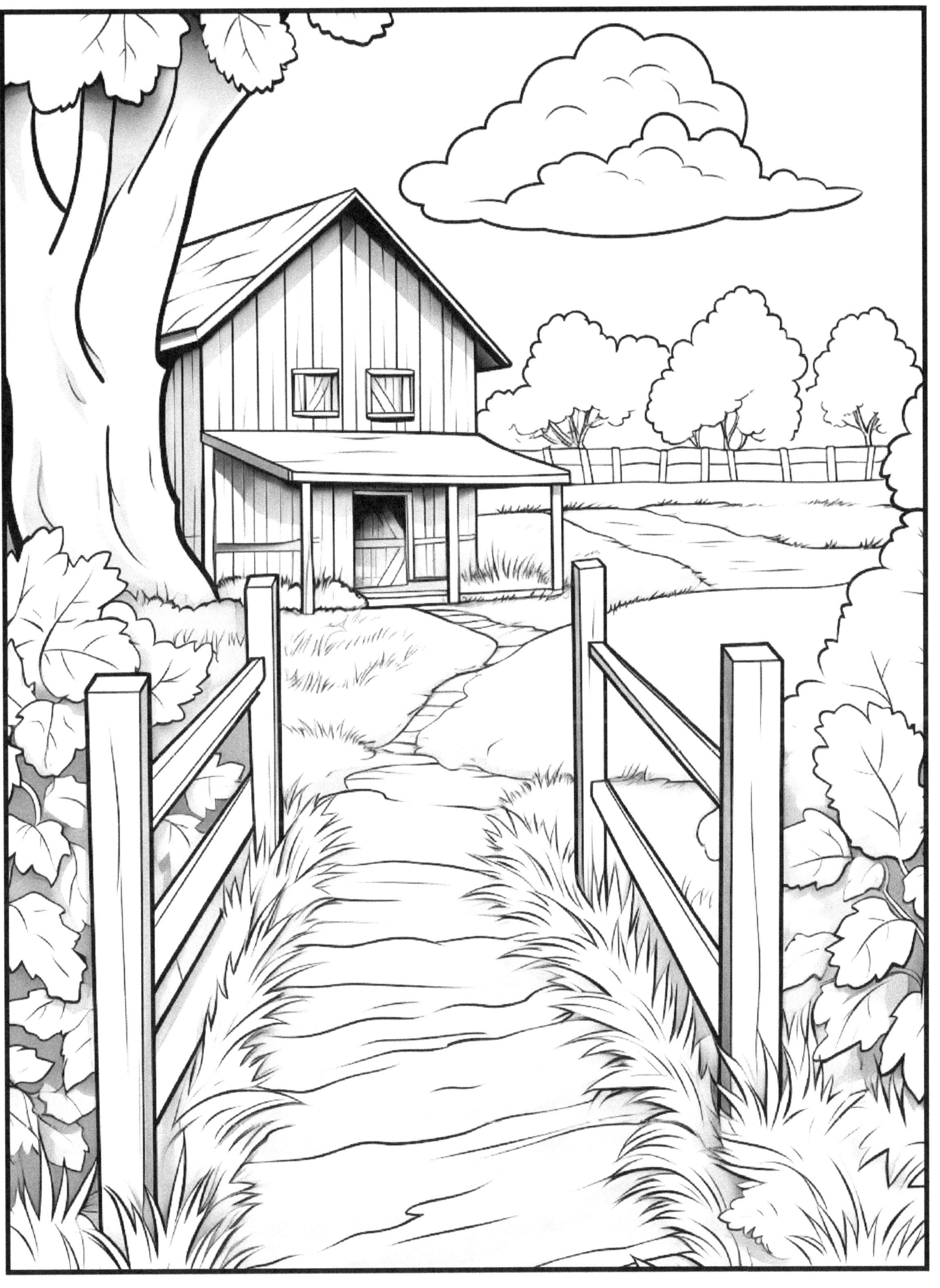

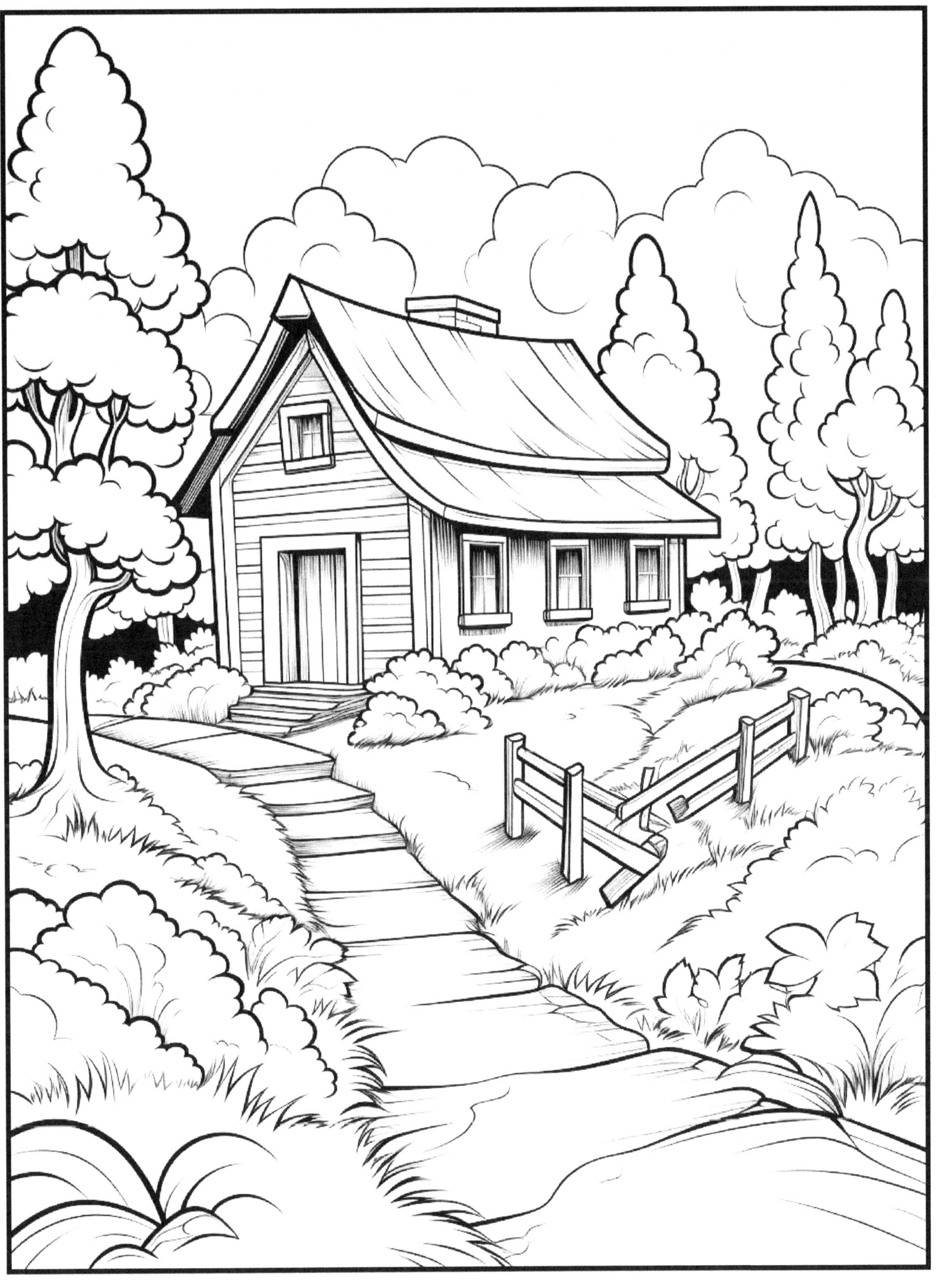

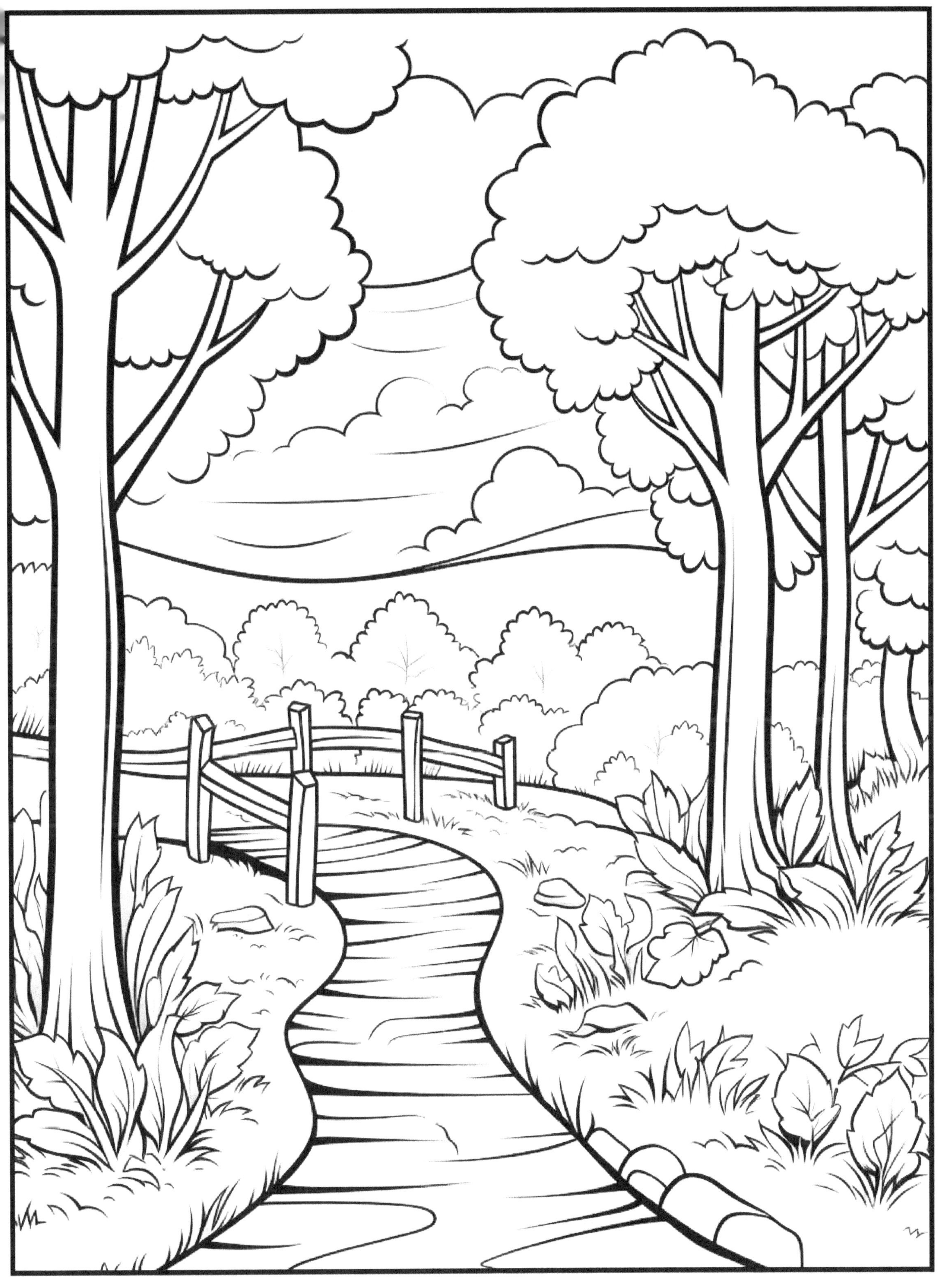

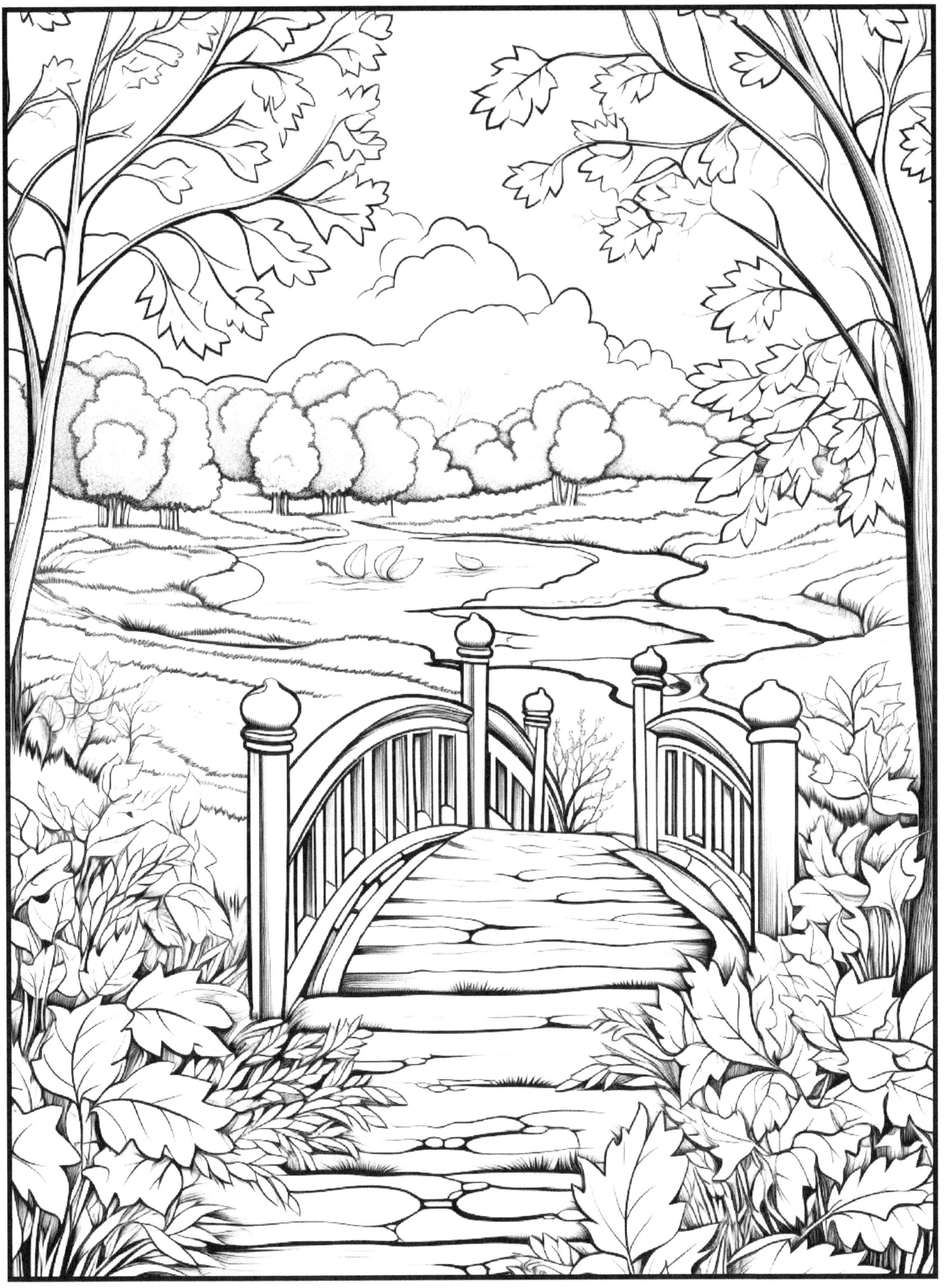

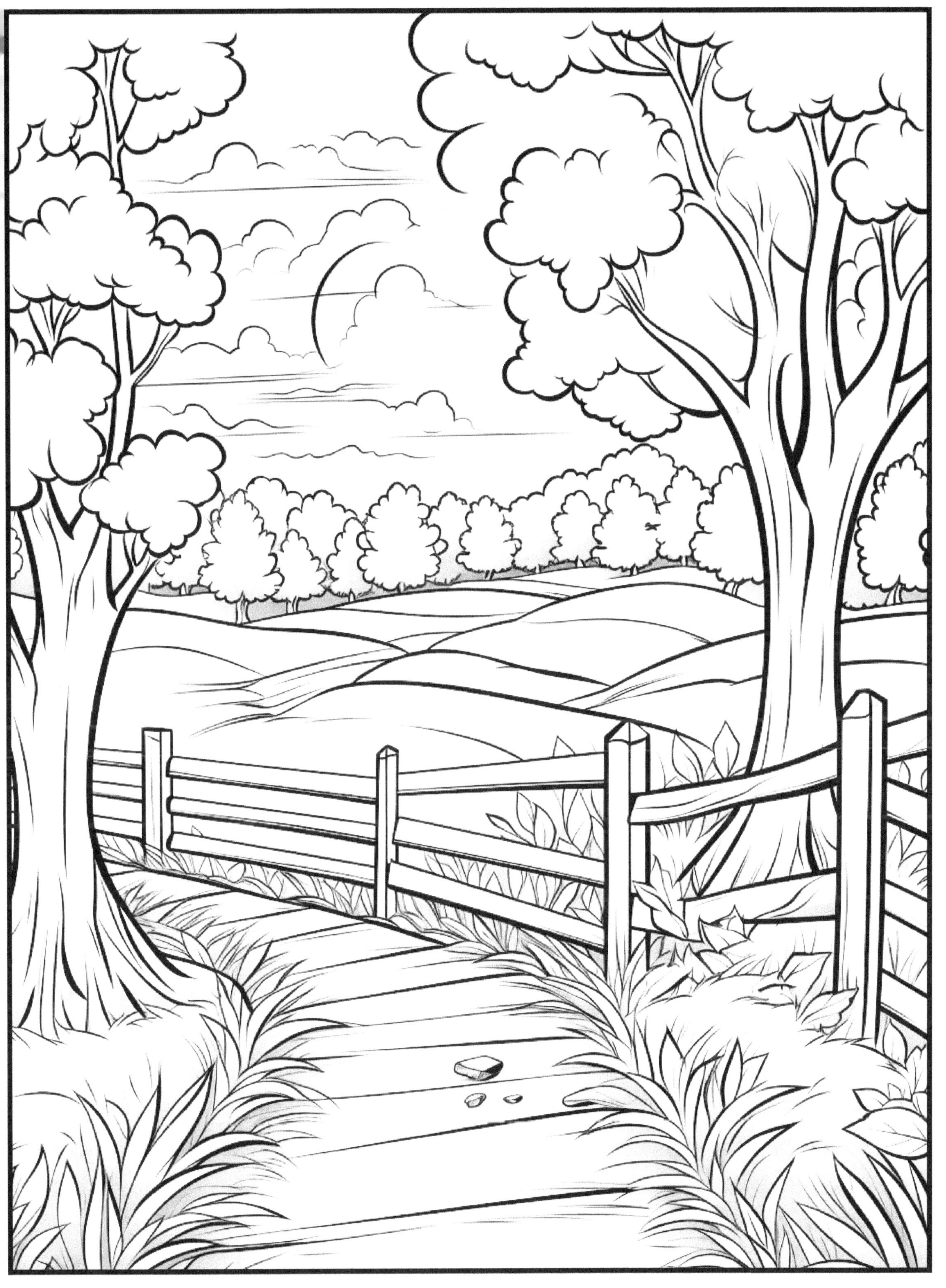

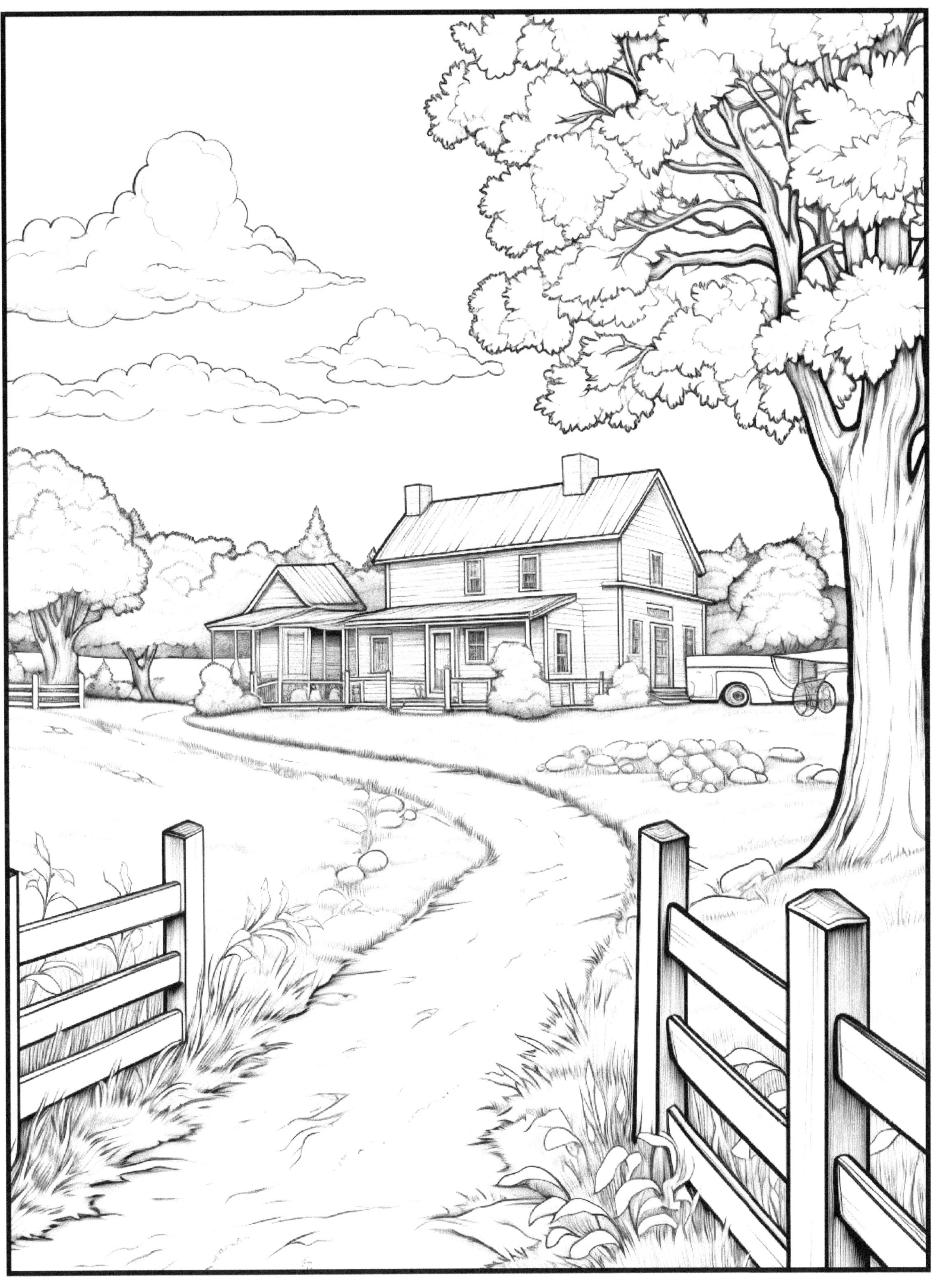

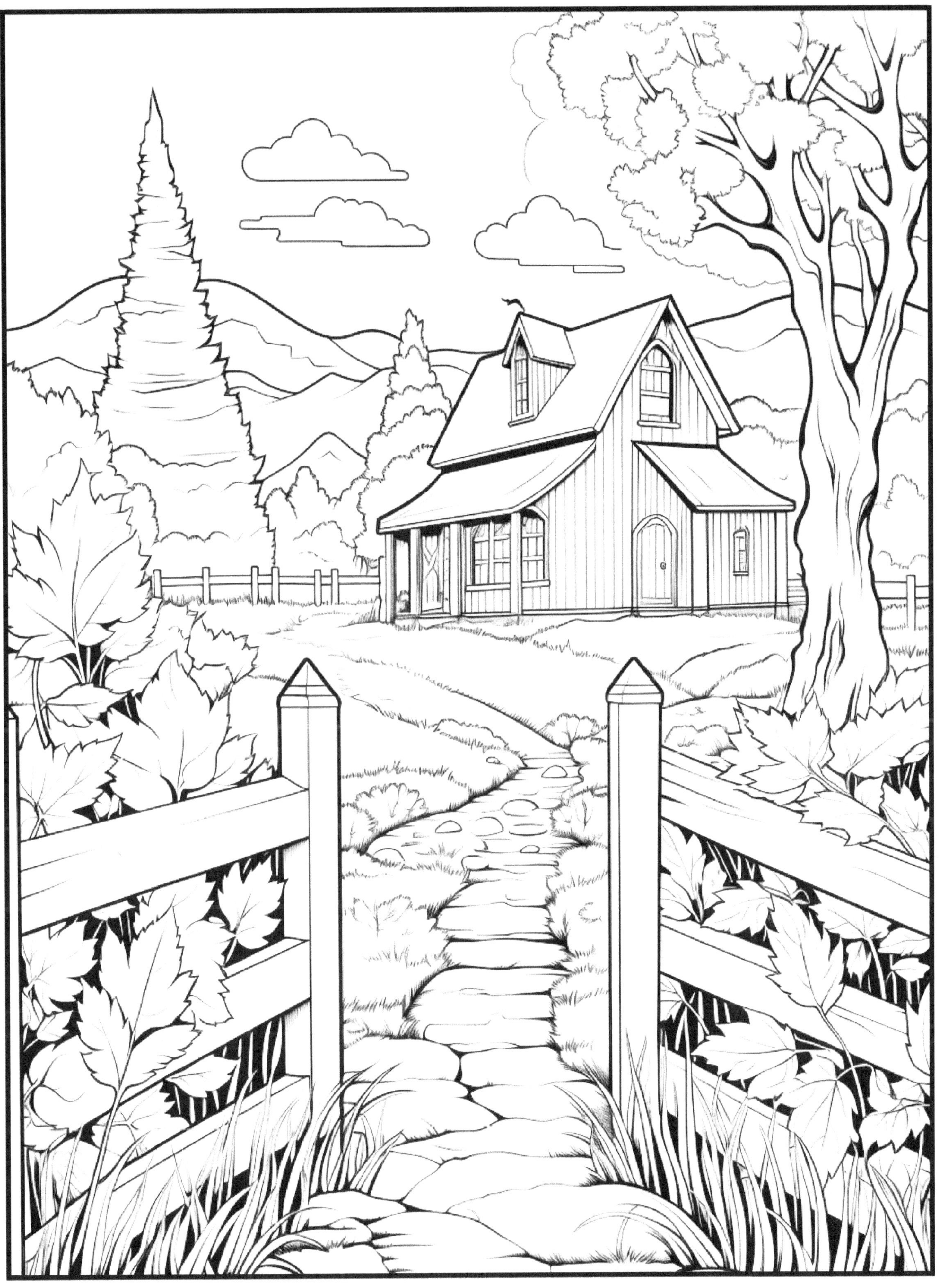

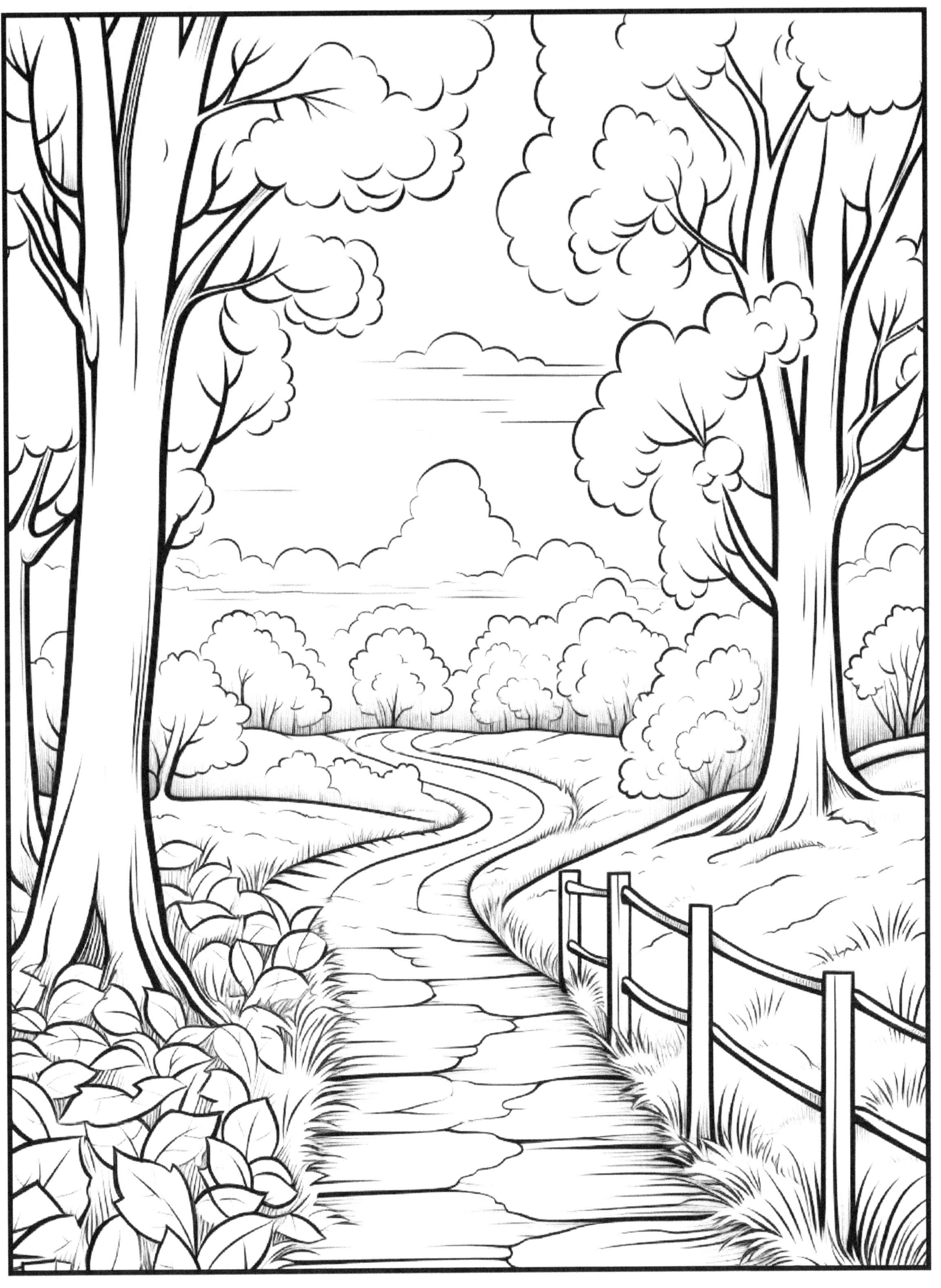

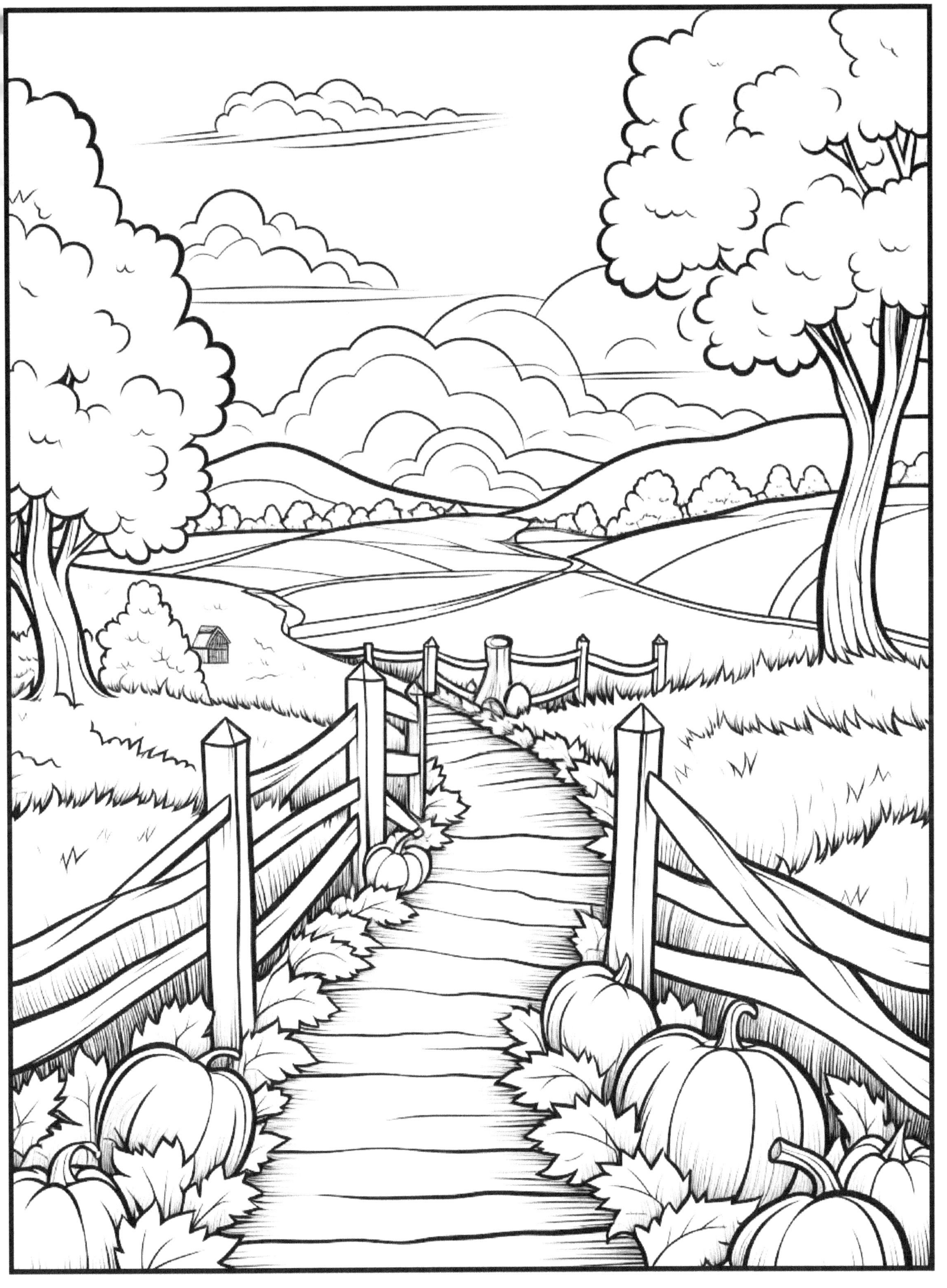

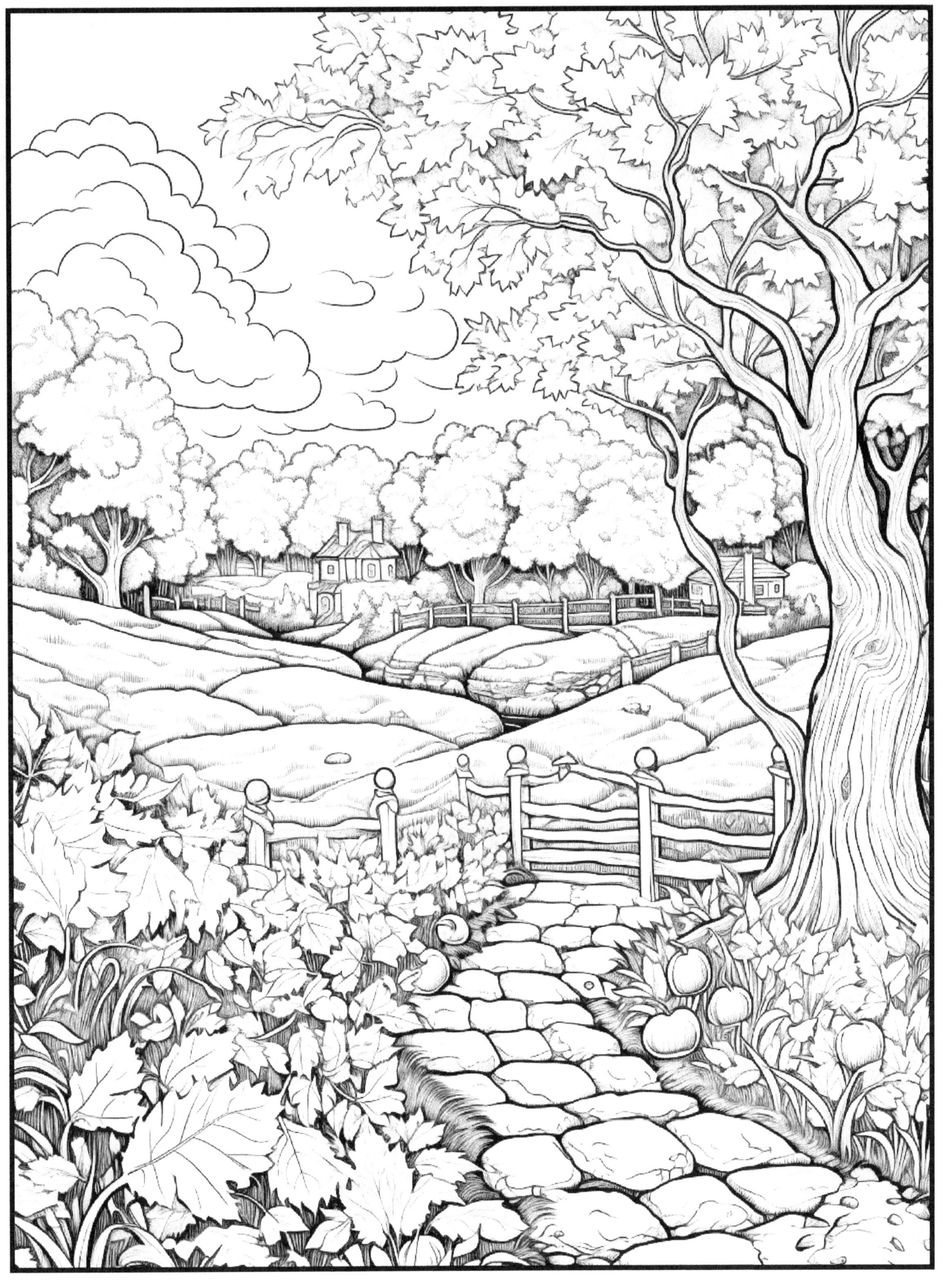

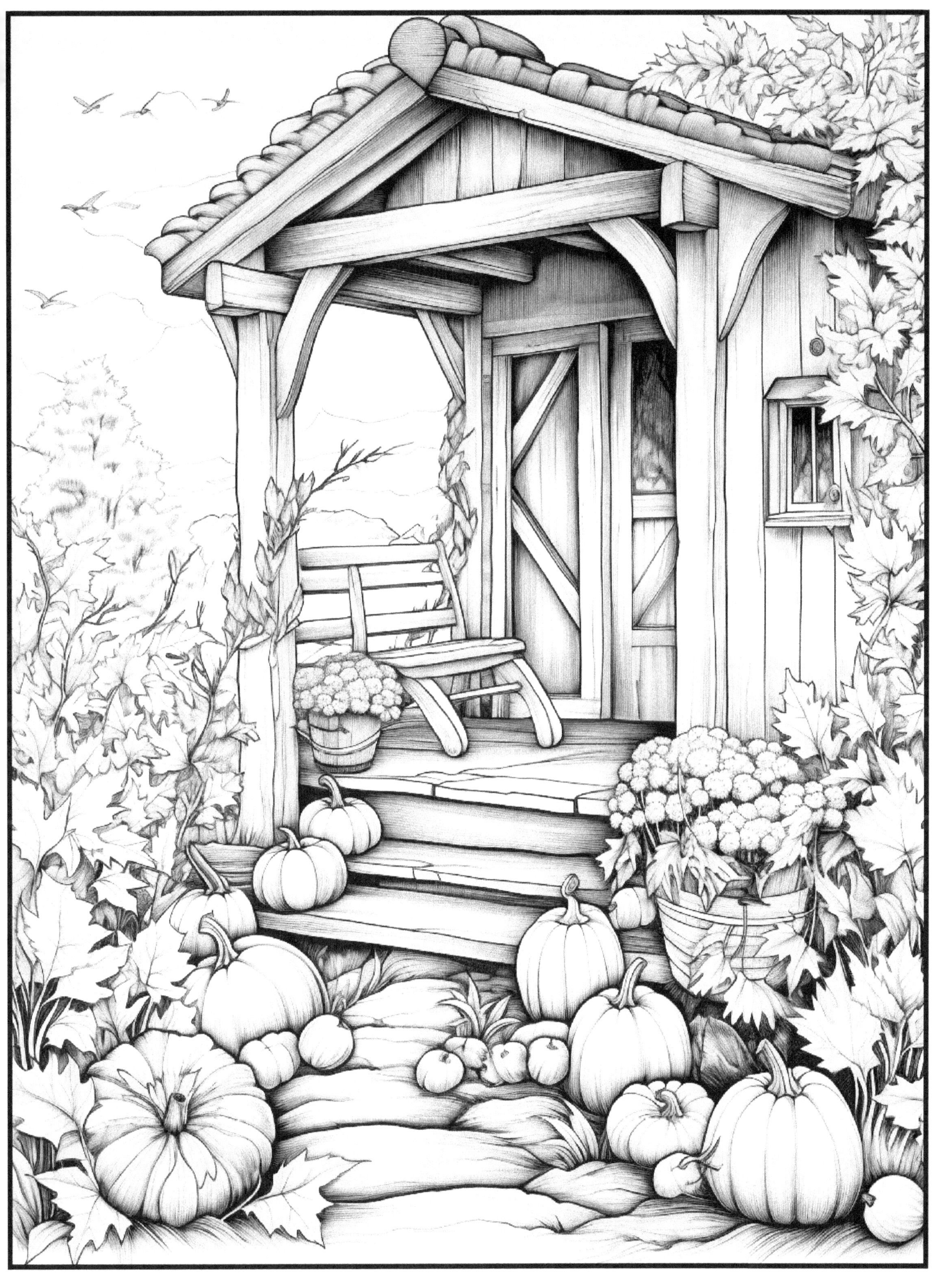

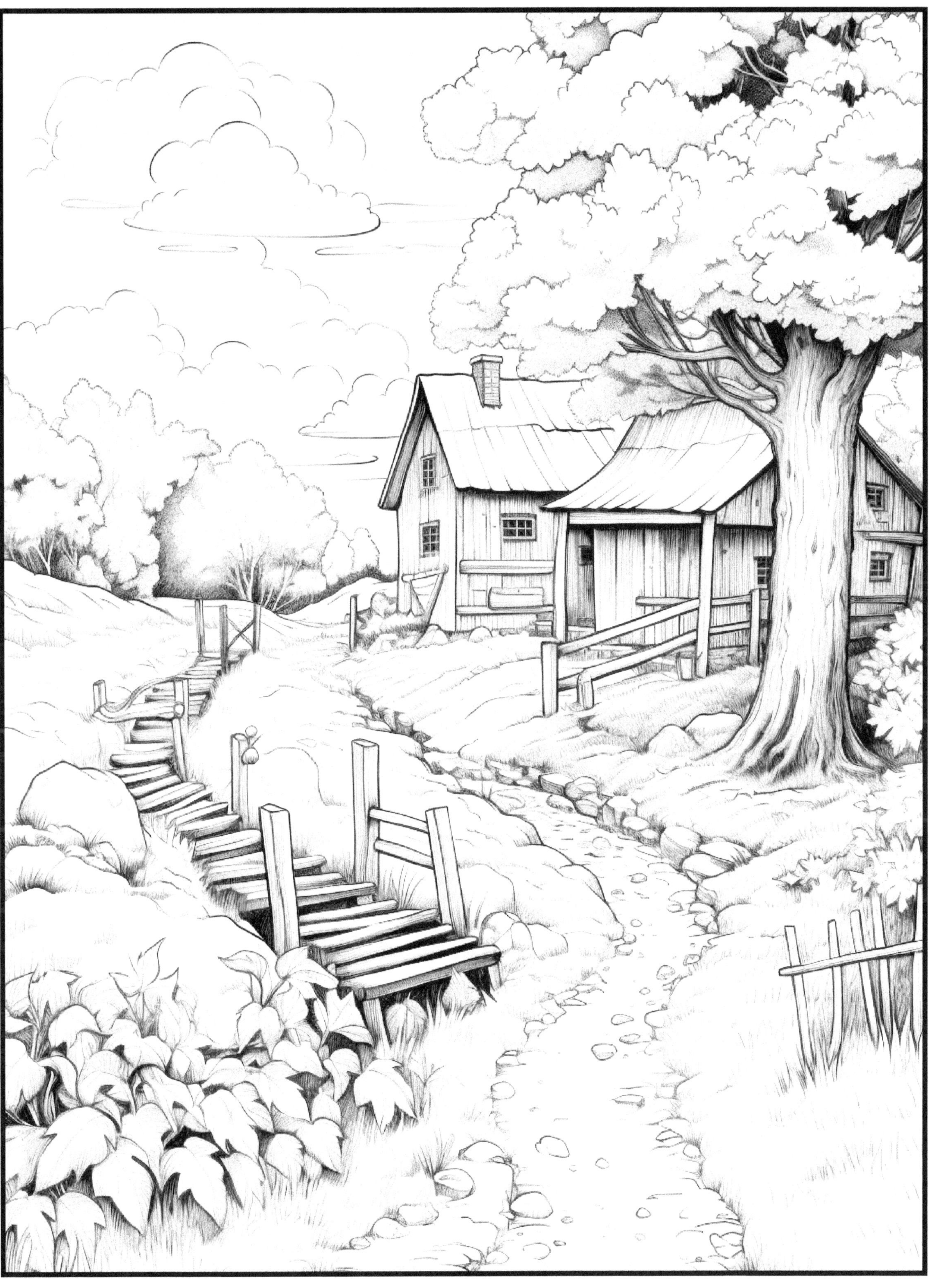

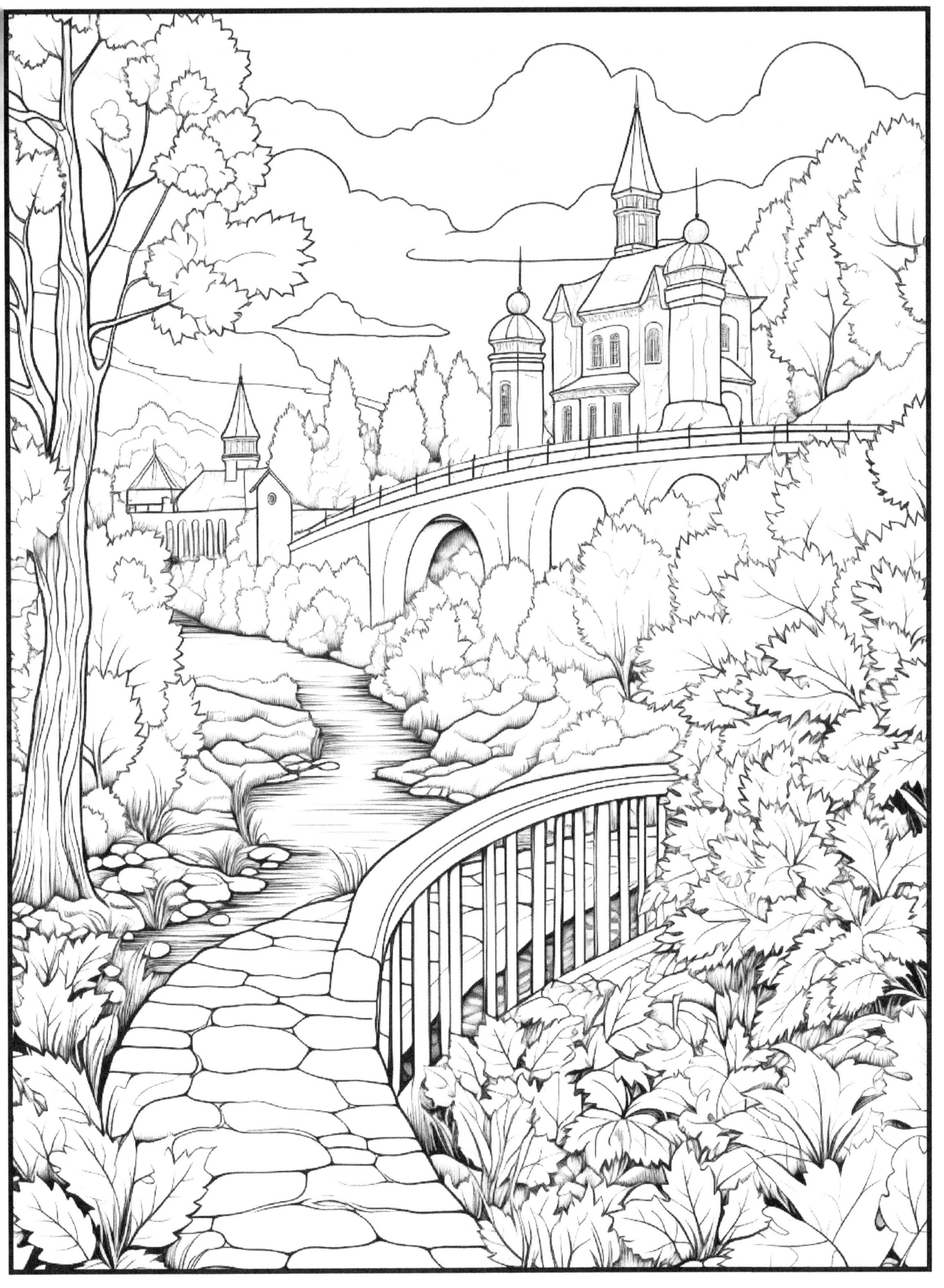

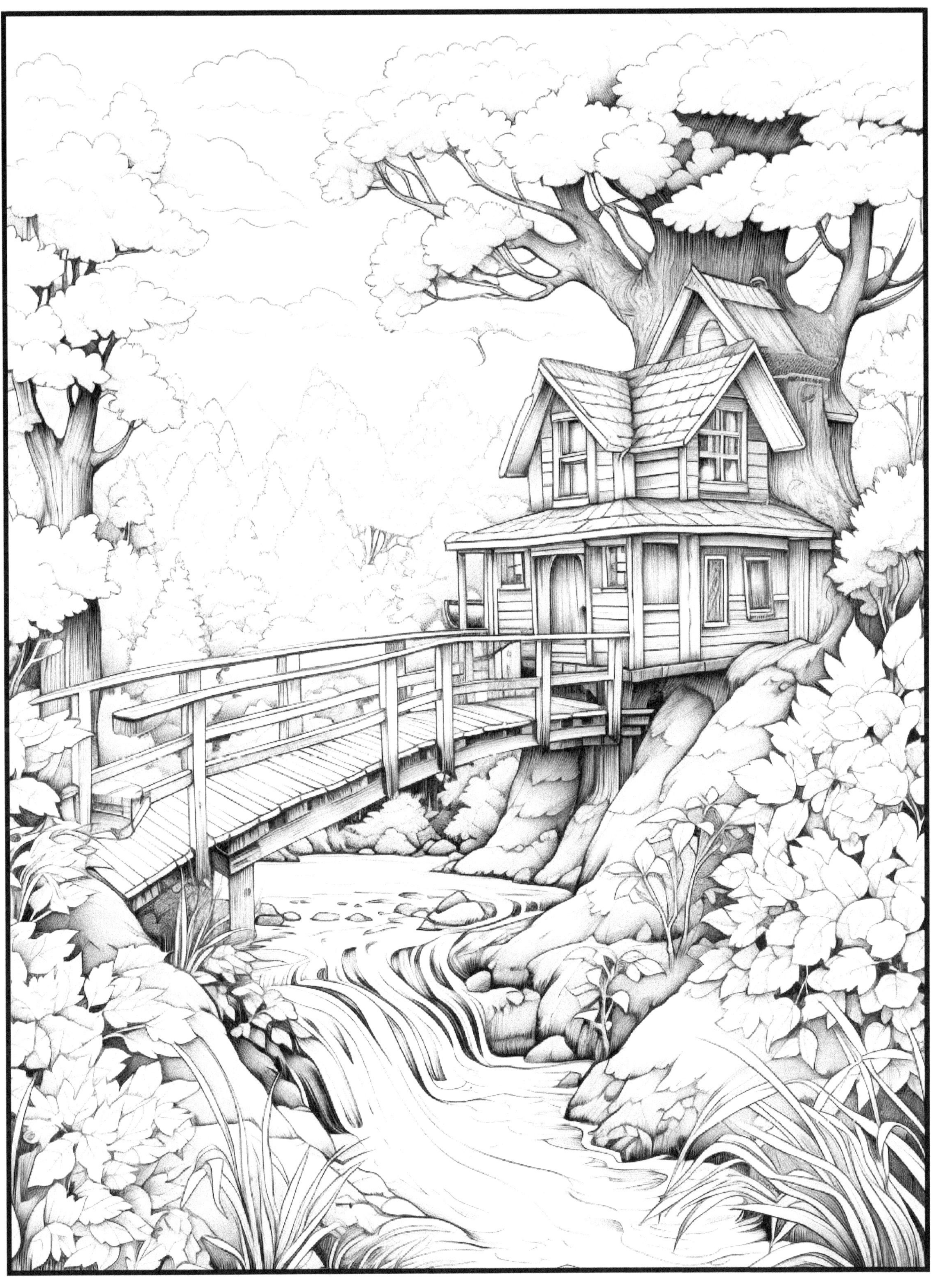

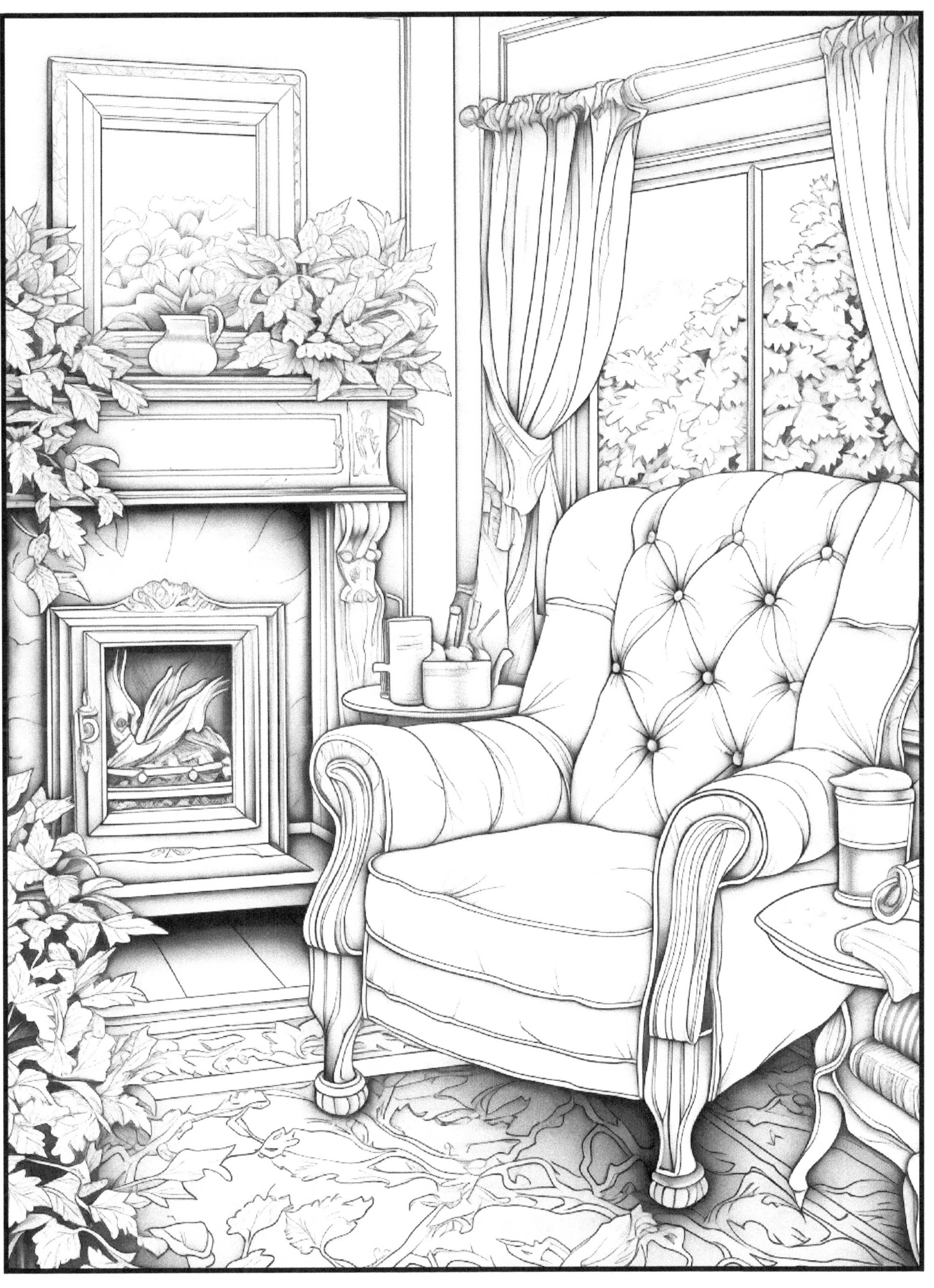

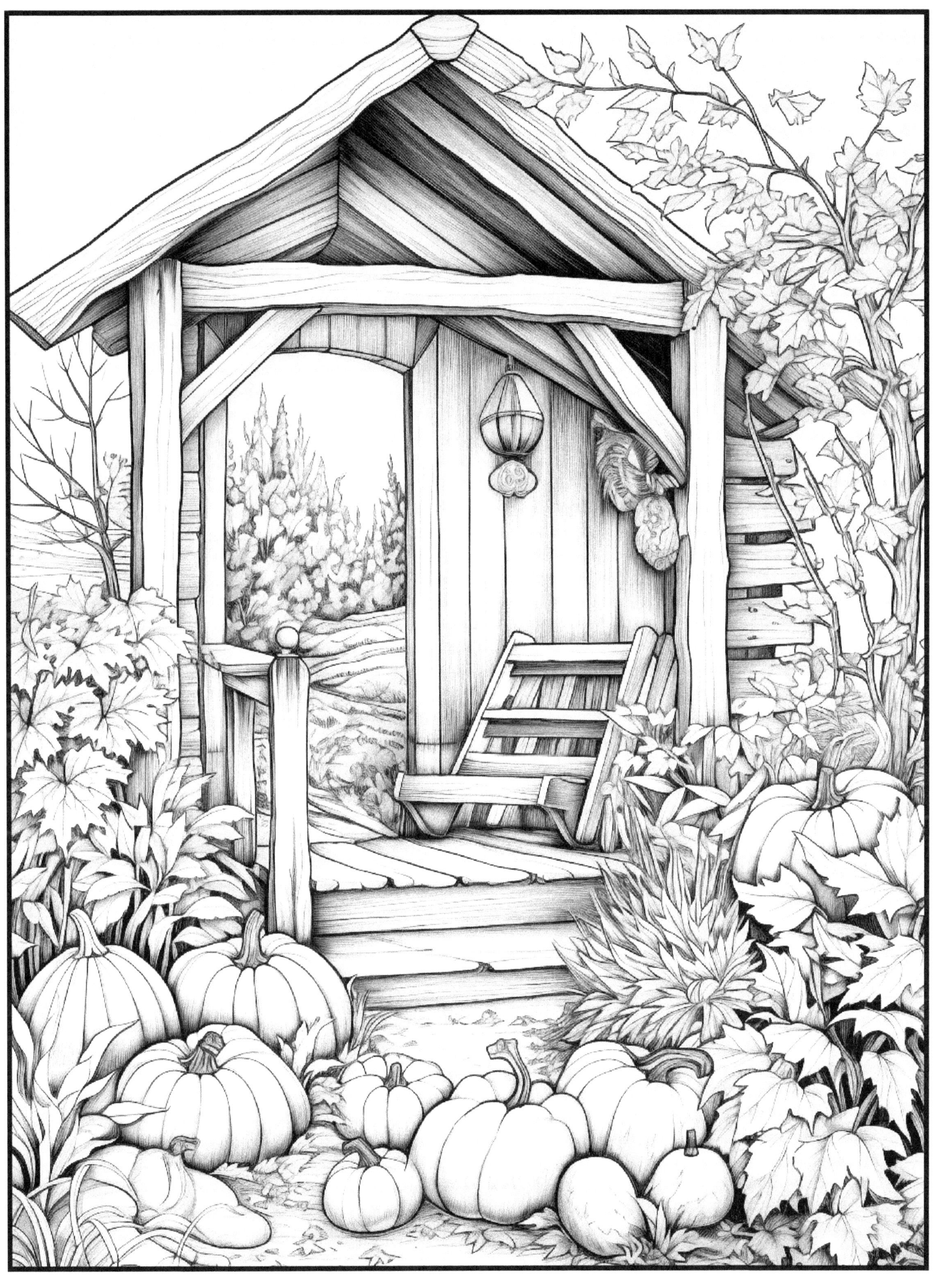

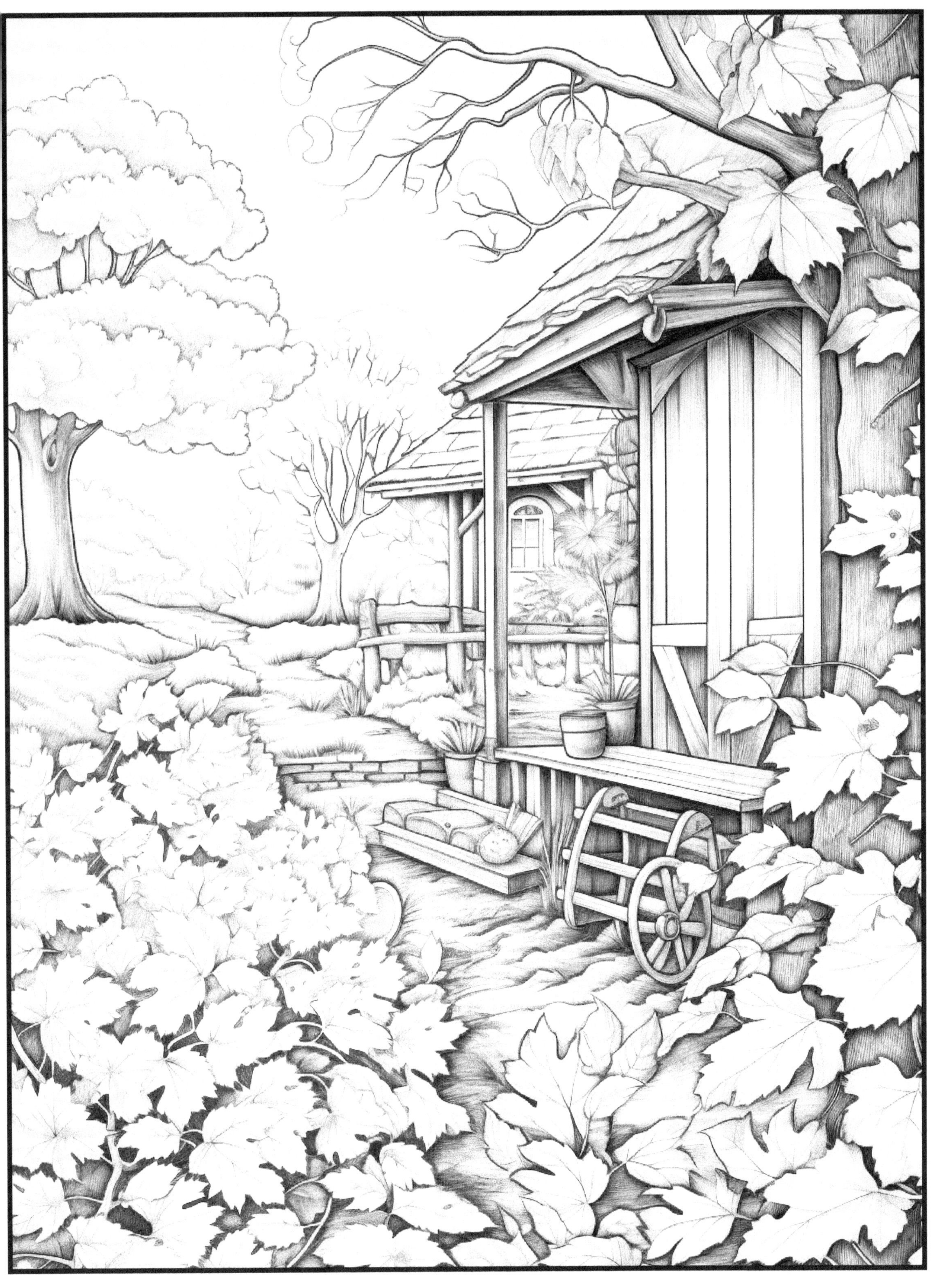

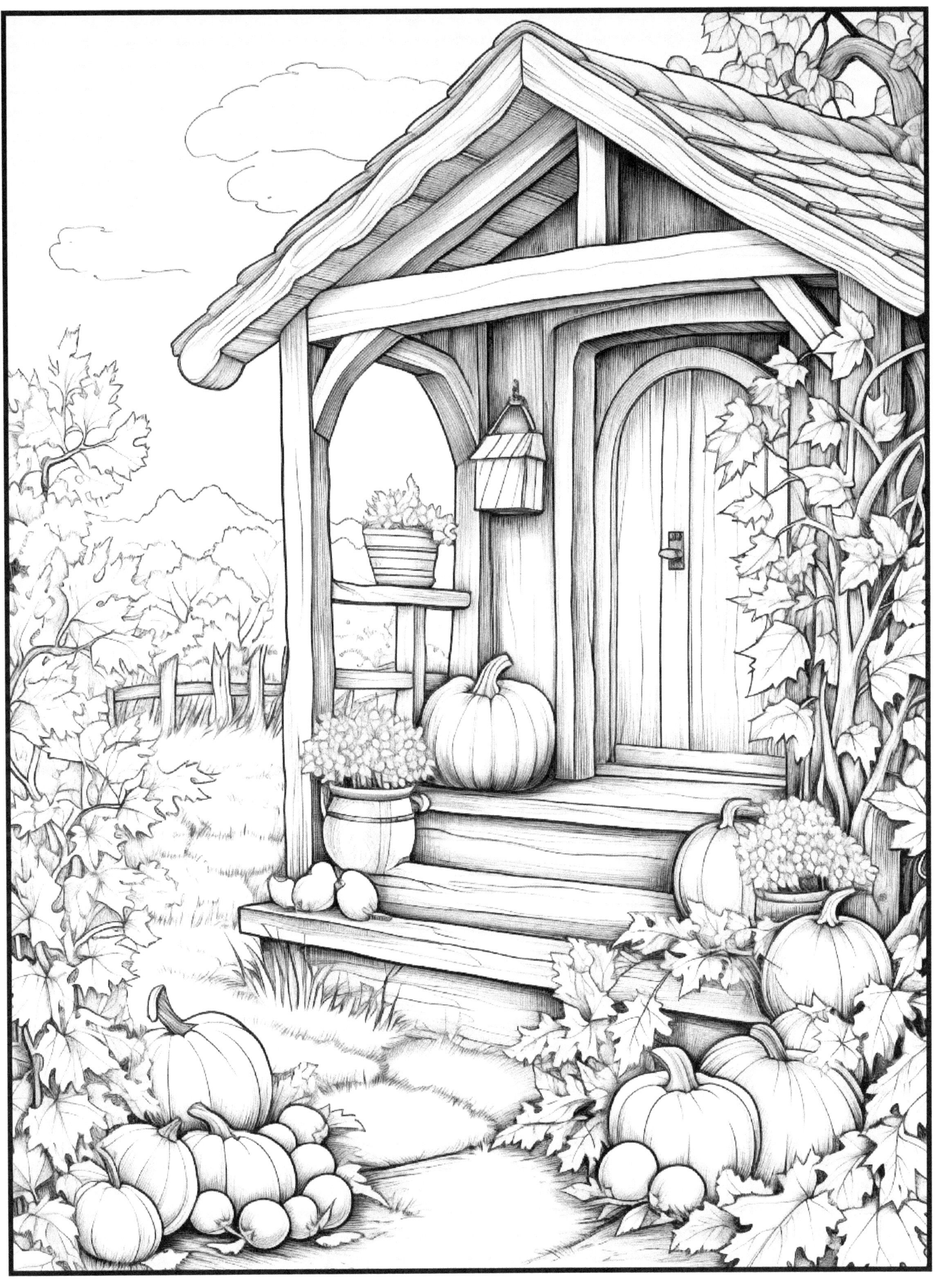

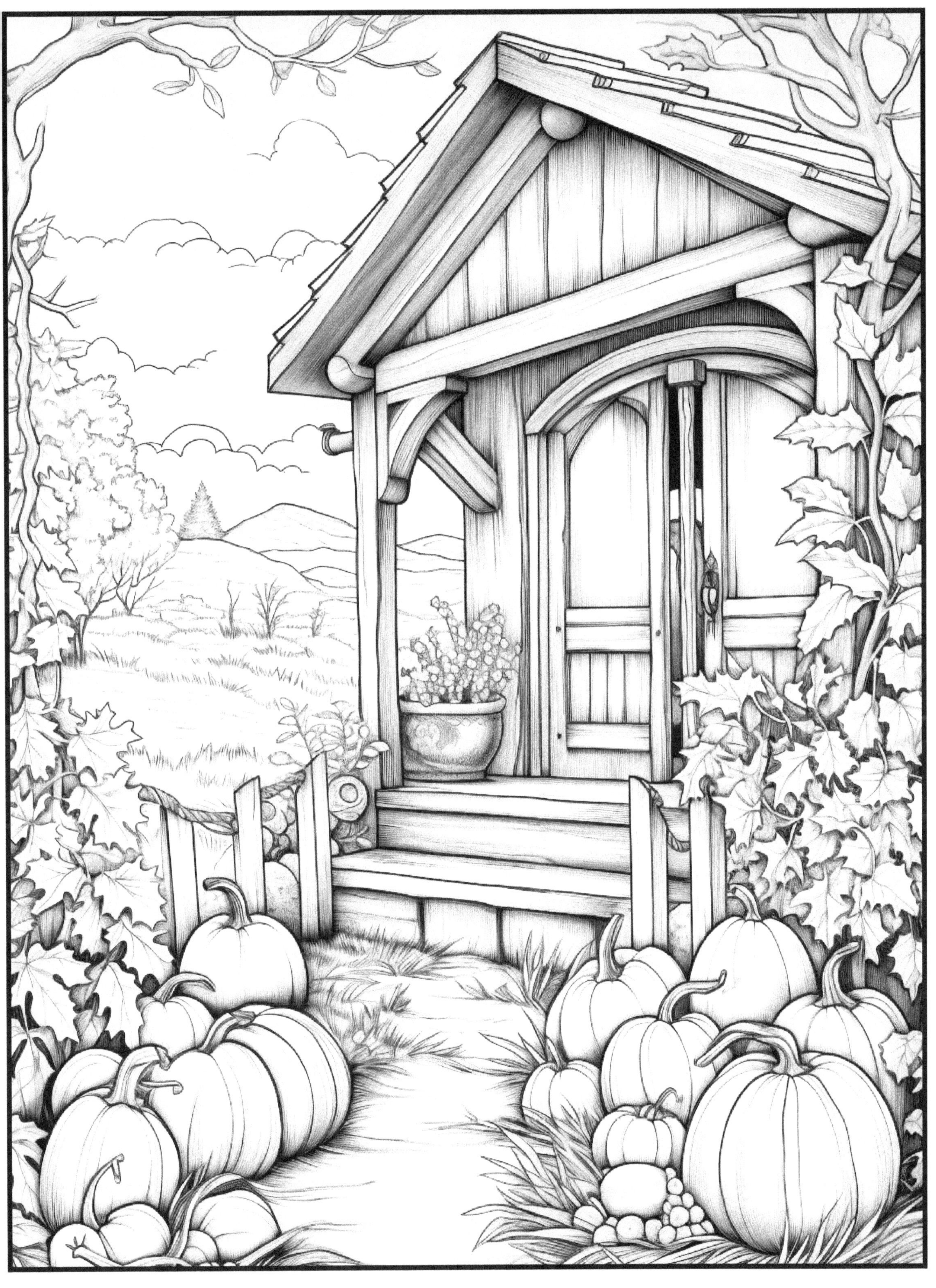